real marriage

Bob,

Blessings

Kelly

real marriage

WHERE FANTASY MEETS REALITY

Kelly & Tosha Williams

TATE PUBLISHING *& Enterprises*

Scripture quotations are taken from the Holy Bible, New Living Translation, Copyright © 1996. Used by permission of Tyndale House Publishers, Inc. All rights reserved.

The opinions expressed by the author are not necessarily those of Tate Publishing, LLC.

Published by Tate Publishing & Enterprises, LLC
127 E. Trade Center Terrace | Mustang, Oklahoma 73064 USA
1.888.361.9473 | www.tatepublishing.com

Tate Publishing is committed to excellence in the publishing industry. The company reflects the philosophy established by the founders, based on Psalm 68:11,
"The Lord gave the word and great was the company of those who published it."

Book design copyright © 2008 by Tate Publishing, LLC. All rights reserved.
Cover design by Summer Harvey
Interior design by Nathan Harmony

Published in the United States of America

ISBN: 978-1-60696-909-0
1. Family and Relationships / Marriage
2. Religion / Christian Life / Love & Marriage
08.10.29

Five children are watching our endeavor to experience REAL marriage. Through the fantasy and reality, these children are the greatest blessing of our marriage.

With love, we dedicate this book to them.

Anastasha Dawnné Joy
You represent "Resurrection Morning Joy" to us.

Christianna Angellen Hope
We believe you are "Christ's Messenger of Hope."

Joshua Kellen Chandler
You are our "Strong Warrior that God has delivered to Bear the Light."

Annalarie McKenzie Faith
You are "Crowned with Honor, Wisdom and Faith" in our eyes.

Annaka Journey Grace
You represent our "Journey of Grace upon Grace."

acknowledgments

Our marriage has been blessed with five children—five noisy, hungry, busy, talkative, crying wonderful children. We love each one of them so much, but we cannot easily write a book and simultaneously care for their needs. We are very grateful to the women who regularly loved on our little ones so that we could complete this manuscript. Nancy Hoyman, Andrea Heisler, Connie Lamdin, Laura Schwarz, Laura Fowler, Laura Clapp, Elisha Wyant and Ellen Goad: thank you for your support along the way with our family.

While our younger children were crying for our attention, our older children were waiting for it. Anastasha, Christianna and Joshua, we know how you *Realized the Cost* and paid it so we could write *REAL Marriage*. Thank you for helping us along the way, by playing with your little sisters, doing chores to keep our household running and waiting patiently for "your turn." We think you are amazing!

We have a friend who has weekly helped us so we could write. From the beginning, she asked that her service to us be confidential. We want to honor her privacy, but we also want her to know how much she has encouraged and blessed us. Dear lady, you are truly a God-send to our lives. Thank you.

To Melanie Dobson, Kathy Buchanan and Candice Covak, we are extremely grateful for your help with this book. Friends like you make our life's story much better to read, in so many ways more than edits and grammar checks. Thank you for your friendship!

About fifty wonderful couples at Vanguard Church joined us in the spring of 2007 for a "small gathering" in which we went through this book. Thank you all for willingly wading through the first draft of this manuscript with us. Your participation, interaction and feedback honored us greatly. We so enjoyed that semester with you, and we appreciate you for investing in this process.

Many people have prayed for us, believed in us and supported us along the way. How grateful we are to be surrounded by friends and family such as you. May you experience the richest of blessings from our Creator.

contents

Section Four–Love Each Other

introduction

Everybody has sex, but not everybody experiences REAL love. The hope of a truly happy marriage seems to be an impossible ambition. After all, we know there is no such thing as a perfect relationship. Still, we desperately want "happily ever after" to be more than just an illusion in our lives. We want our reality to include some fantasy. We want our stories to rise above the mundane and read of romance, connection and intimacy.

This in mind, one wintry evening—the night of our sixteenth dating anniversary—the two of us began the process of writing the book you are now holding. At a coffee shop that night, we overheard a few twenty-something single women who were sipping lattes. They chatted about getting married someday, what their weddings would be like and who would get married first. Interests tweaked, we took the liberty to introduce ourselves and ask them what one thing they would most like to know about marriage.

We were not presuming we could answer that question, but we wanted to know what their pressing issues were. Unanimously, they responded that they would like to know if it was possible for marriage to last. They wondered whether they should live together to find out if they were compatible.

Is there a DNA test that can show that you and your partner are meant for each other? Is there a lifetime marriage gene that you need to make sure your lover has before marrying that person? How *do* you know how to pick somebody in your twenties that you will still want to be with in your thirties and forties? How *can* you tell if the person you are dating is really your soul mate?

And, once you are married, how does that person remain your soul mate? What you want in life changes sometimes. Your spouse may or may not. When life changes, there are new demands and challenges. The realities of life are overwhelming. What do you do? How do you navigate it all? These quandaries cause many people to give up on love and marriage.

Like those young women, many of us in a post-modern, post-God, post-happily-ever-after society are cynical about marriage. We may enter marriage naïve, thinking romance will last. However, we quickly become jaded when the realities of life bombard us. We end up losing our confidence in marriage's ability to bring happiness to our lives. We give up on the hope of experiencing something spectacular in marriage.

If, by some chance, we see a marriage that not only lasts but also is unusually happy, we are shocked. *How does that*

Kelly and Tosha Williams

happen? Our generation is confused and bewildered about how to experience REAL love that lasts a lifetime.

That cold Colorado evening, we began to brainstorm the ideas we set forth in this book. "Happily ever after" may seem more and more unattainable with every passing decade, but it does not have to be impossible. We are holding out hope that love can last and marriage can be amazing. The way to experience that, we believe, is through REAL.

In our society, "real" is a cliché about being vulnerable, honest or transparent. This can be helpful in relationship, but it is only the starting point. We believe that real can be, and should be, much more than that. The REAL we describe in this book is all about that "more." It is about where fantasy meets reality.

We believe that REAL can affect your marriage for the better because it did that for our marriage. During the months it took for us to write the ideas in *REAL Marriage*, our relationship profoundly changed. After almost fourteen years of marriage, the concepts were a jump-start for every part of our relationship. This was not always an easy process, yet the investment in our marriage has been so worth it.

By the fact that you are reading this book, we know that you want to invest in your marriage, too. Maybe you are engaged right now, or perhaps you will soon celebrate your fourteenth wedding anniversary like us. Perhaps you want to find love with your partner like you have never before experienced, or maybe you want to rekindle what you used to have with your spouse. Whoever you are, whatever your circumstances, you are holding out hope that love and marriage *can* last and *can* be REAL.

Even though we do not personally know you, we believe in your marriage. We share pages of our story because we sincerely desire for you to experience REAL marriage in the chapters of your life, too. This does not mean we have a perfect relationship—far from it! But we are learning things that can make as much of a difference in your marriage as they have in ours.

Trust us, there will be pain involved in this process. However, as we have learned, pain does not kill the dream of REAL love. Pain simply purifies the love and proves whether it is REAL. The lovers—you and your spouse—choose whether to allow your love to live on or die. As you will see in the pages to come, you get to choose how fantasy and reality dance in your marriage.

If you want this book to make a difference in your marriage, we suggest that you read it slowly. It took us months to process and internalize the concepts of *REAL Marriage*. We encourage you to take the time to do the same. Make a plan for both of you to read a chapter a week or every other week, then have a date night or conversation time together to process the information and answer the questions before you go on to the next chapter.

We suggest that you type or write your answers because these are the pages of *your* book. This may seem like a lot of effort, but it is a strategic investment in your marriage. If you do this, you will create a powerful journal of who you are as a couple. This is something you will come back to again and again. Please do not skip any of the pages and chapters of *your* story.

Kelly and Tosha Williams

Are you ready to begin the journey of REAL? Are you ready for your fantasy to meet your reality like never before?

Then turn the page, brace yourself, release your heart and explore with us the experience of *REAL Marriage*.

Section One:

Realize the Cost

1. the fantasy

"When I first met Katie ... there was an instant connection, this simpatico.
I felt like she just got me. And, believe me, there is no greater feeling in this world than to feel gotten."
- Ben in The Story of Us

Every great fairytale has fantasy. A beautiful princess, caught like a damsel in distress, is under a spell cast upon her by an evil sorcerer. She waits from the top of an abandoned castle as alligators swim in the moat and dragons fly in the air. Isolated from the real world, the princess dreams of her Prince Charming who will sweep her away with loving kisses and break the spell.

As the proverbial fairytale goes, when the beautiful princess catches the imagination of the handsome prince, he leaps onto his horse and rides like the wind to rescue his damsel before the spell destroys her. He arrives just in time to set her free from the impending danger. With one swift strike, he destroys the overwhelming obstacles that stand in the way of his true love. He liberates the woman of his dreams, and the pair lives happily ever after.

Ahhh. Every great fairytale has fantasy.

Every great marriage has fantasy, too.

Fantasy Defined

Your fantasy may not include a princess with long hair or a knight in shining armor, but you *have* dreamed about something grand in love. At one point or another in life, we all have had a fantasy of what we would like love to look like. What is your fantasy? Do you know?

Since you are reading this book, we assume you are either married or getting married. That being the case, what do you think marriage should be? What do love and fantasy look like in your relationship? Are you experiencing it?

Now, you might have grown up learning that fantasy is evil, selfish, something you keep to yourself, a secret that only you know, something you take to your grave. We beg to differ. Certainly, distorted fantasy can be those things. Yet, in its purest sense, fantasy is something far greater than you may have imagined up to this point for your marriage.

The primary definition of fantasy in Webster's dictionary is "the free play of creative imagination." Simply put, fantasy is an invention. In your marriage, fantasy is your invention and your spouse's invention. It is something *you* imagine and give your marriage the freedom to create.

For the sake of your marriage, you need to know that good, healthy fantasy exists, or else you will not experience it. You must be able to create a fantasy in order to experience it. In order to create it, you must be able to imagine it. So, what is your imagination about a fairytale marriage? What have you always hoped to experience with your spouse?

In our relationship, we choose to think of fantasy as *our creative ways to stay deeply connected to one another*. There are also other ways to describe healthy, marriage-building fantasy:

- Fantasy is a great love, a marriage that goes the distance.
- Fantasy is a romance that reaches the heights, weathers the storms and survives the fires.
- Fantasy is a passionate relationship that lasts for a lifetime.
- Fantasy is not all about sex, but it sure includes some great sex.
- Fantasy is being "gotten" by somebody who knows you deeply.
- Fantasy is about your hopes and dreams, your goals and desires in a relationship with the one you vowed to spend your life with.
- Fantasy is essential to having life in marriage.

From the time we are children until we become adults, we all have our personal wishes and dreams. Somewhere between childhood fantasies and adult responsibility, though, we quit dreaming about some things. Unfortunately, our marriages do not escape the demise of our dreams. As reality sets in, we succumb to the pressures, the responsibilities and the duties. Along the way, our fantasies drift off to sea, seemingly never to be desired, experienced or rediscovered again.

It does not have to be this way. If you are married, we bet that, at some point, you dreamed about a fairytale life. You dreamed about your knight in shining armor or your beautiful princess. We did. Our dreams and wishes did not evolve out of thin air, though, and neither did yours. Your fantasy—what you desire in a relationship—grows out of the story of your life. This story is important because you are always coming back to it. Somehow, the earlier chapters weave their way into later chapters.

We invite you to journey back with us to the enchanted forests of our childhood and adolescence as we recount the beginnings of our romantic fantasies. As you read these sketches of our travels, we want you to think about your own journey. What did you hope for? What did *you* dream about for a great love? Are you experiencing that?

Kelly's Fantasy

It all began for me in first grade when I saw Nikki across the room. She was beautiful, and I wanted her to be my girlfriend. As the first day of school wore on, I talked my two new buddies into helping me pester the heck out of Nikki on the playground. This was the beginning of my romantic fantasies which would one day culminate at the altar with my wife.

I do not remember much about those first few years of grade school, but I do remember waking up one morning, looking in the mirror and saying to myself, "I need to comb

Kelly and Tosha Williams

my hair." It was fourth grade, and I was in love. With whom? It did not matter; what mattered was that I looked good. From that day forth, I vowed to make my hair the project of my morning so that when I went to school I could wow the girls. I think I used about a can of hair spray each day as I set my 1970's feathered-back look in place. I was quite impressed with my efforts, and I was sure the girls would be as well.

With my new hairstyle and incredible ability to write love notes, I just knew that I was going to be the number one ladies' man. Yeah, love was tough, and relationships rarely lasted more than a day, but I felt I was getting the hang of this love thing and doing quite well.

It was not until sixth grade that I met the love of my childhood. She came to our small country school from another country, and she was exotically different from all the other girls. Although I had a girlfriend or two at the time, this new girl swept me off my feet. She was athletic, pretty, smart and fun. I knew then that I would marry her and that we would live happily ever after.

Sorry to say, she broke my heart. Even though we liked each other off and on during junior high, she dropped me for an older guy once we hit high school. I went on to date other girls, but, secretly, she remained the dream of my heart. It was not until I went off to college that her pull on my heartstrings began to loosen.

The first day of college, I was standing in line waiting to check in when I spotted a gorgeous girl who I was determined to ask out on a date. I thought to myself, "Maybe she's the one!" When I got a chance to date her, though, I discovered I was not as impressed as I thought I would be. She was pretty, but she was also dull.

Somewhere along the way, in the midst of going out with my supposed dream date and others, I met Tosha. I must confess that she did not register a blip on my radar.

Nonetheless, at some point I was smitten by her without even knowing it. Over Christmas break, when I was home in Kentucky, I had a conversation with my mother about love and relationship. My mom and I were very close, so I trusted her thoughts on such weighty matters. When I mentioned Tosha, I told my mother that, although I was not interested in dating her, I could not quit thinking about her. To my surprise, my mother commented, "You'll probably marry her one day." This was not the response I wanted. I returned to school after the break determined to go out with Tosha on one date, take her off my list and get her off my mind.

There was nothing wrong with Tosha. She was pretty, kind, gentle and very caring. Yet, at that time in college, I was looking for a girl who was irresistible, unattainable, overtly sexually appealing and challenging to my ego. Tosha was not the woman of my dreams I had envisioned.

Unfortunately, I had fallen in love with an idea that did not exist. My fantasy idea of the woman I would spend the rest of my life with was one shaped largely by that teenage relationship I could not have. Don't we always want we cannot have? I know I did. I knew Tosha would say *yes* if I asked her out, and this made her unappealing to me.

Unfortunately, my fantasy ideal of a woman was also shaped by a different teenage relationship that I had. In my last year of high school, I dated a girl who, though I was not too interested in, became my girlfriend. About this same time, partly because of the other rejection in dating and partly because of the lack of success in sports, I had come to the point that I was interested—very interested—in experimenting sexually.

One night I decided to lose my virginity. A few hours later, I found myself parked on a dark road making out with this girl in my truck. Fortunately, before we had sex, I came to my senses, told her I did not want to destroy our lives and took her home. The relationship ended, but it awakened within me physical passions that I could not deny or even define. When I went off to college, I was determined to land the woman that no one, not even she, thought I could get and impress everyone else in the process. Furthermore, in the back of mind, there were physical characteristics that mattered to me more than anything else did.

With all this in my head, I found myself going into college confused, as many people are at that time about relationships and, especially, romantic relationships. I overlooked Tosha as long as I could. Nonetheless, along the way, through casual dates and conversations, I discovered a woman far more confident than I first detected; far more unattainable than I thought; far more challenging to my ego that I could have imagined; and much more desirable and sexually appealing than I had first reckoned. Actually, I remember at one point thinking to myself, "She is intimidating to me." I remember another time when I went into my dorm room, fell flat on my bed and said aloud, "She's pretty!"

Why did I not notice these things about her at first? I could not have answered that question many years ago, but I think I can now. Our early dates led into a three-year dating relationship during which my fantasy of a woman began to change. Up to this time, I had primarily seen a woman from a one-dimensional point of view that was, unfortunately, overtly sexual. Even though I had never been with a woman sexually, my mind looked primarily through that lens, giving very little credence to any other ideal. Sure, I thought about other virtues in a woman, but mostly I thought about sex appeal.

Truthfully, when I met Tosha, I could not even think of her in a physical way, and that somehow scared me and made me not even want to be around her. Nevertheless, I could not get her off my mind so, week after week, I kept asking her out.

As time went on, I discovered that fantasy is about much more than sex, though sex is certainly a part of the equation. Good fantasy is holistic. It does not just start and stop with the body; it entails the body, mind, spirit *and* soul. In the process of dating Tosha, my thoughts on dating and relationship changed. I learned how important verbal communication is to stay connected emotionally. I also discovered the beauty of spirituality in a way that I did not even know existed.

By the time I went home from college to work four months before getting married, my fantasies were alive and well. They were affecting every part of me: soul, mind, spirit *and* body. I longed for my future wife, a spiritual woman who could communicate emotionally and physically. I could not wait to have her body that I could feast upon to my sexual soul's content. I was hot for my future wife.

We counted down the days from 100 until we could be together forever. Every day, my fantasy grew. My heart beat for hers. My soul longed to be one with her. I could not wait

Kelly and Tosha Williams

to be married to the woman of my dreams and live happily ever after in her arms.

Tosha's Fantasy

Kelly may have fallen in love for the first time in first grade, but I met the loves of my life in kindergarten. Yes, *loves,* plural: Kenny and Timothy. I could not decide which of them I liked best, so I had two boyfriends. I am not sure what they thought about me; I cannot imagine that either of them enjoyed sharing the attention of the little girl with pigtails. Still, I thought that one boy was cute and the other was very handsome, and I stayed in love with both of them until my family moved when I was in the second grade.

Then I met Steve. He swept me off my feet by his penchant for rock collecting and our mutual adoration of the Matterhorn at Disney Land. Our families vacationed together, so we spent lots of time together away from school. At family camp one summer, I had my first truly romantic experience with a boy. Steve took me out on a misty pond early one morning for a rowboat ride. He sat on one end of the boat and rowed while I sat on the other end and enjoyed the beautiful morning and good company. I remember our parents laughing about how his wish was my command. My own parents actually seemed to enjoy me having a "boyfriend."

Alas, my young heart broke when my family moved once again, and my boyfriend was left far behind. My affections rebounded by the seventh grade, though, when new love interests appeared. Relationships were the main topic of conversation back then. I remember bouncing on the trampoline with my best girlfriend, both of us dreaming about whom we would marry someday. My boyfriend, Mike, seemed a good possibility, and then Rodney captured my heart. Up to this point, love had been fun and games; now, my junior high mind was thinking more in terms of what love should really be like. Hopes and dreams began to fill my heart; ideals and desires began to sift through my imagination.

Before anything could get too serious, though, my family moved again. I grieved for months the loss of the man of my dreams. When the letters my love had promised never came, his memory eventually faded, but the question did not. Throughout high school, I contemplated the man of my dreams. What would he be like? What *should* he be like?

To my chagrin at the time, I did not have much of an opportunity to find him in high school. The few dates I went out on never materialized into relationships, probably for at least a couple of reasons. Back in middle school, I had decided not to engage physically with a guy on a date. Judging by the parties I was not invited to and Friday nights I spent with my family, word of that standard must have made its way around my new school.

I think that another reason that a relationship never materialized was that no guy could ever begin to live up to the fantasy I had created in my mind. Pragmatically, I did not care to waste my time on someone who was not my dream man, but, practically, I grieved on many lonely Friday nights. I was popular enough in high school, involved in student government, the cheerleading squad, the drama team and other things. My grades put me at the top of the class, and

I had all sorts of friends. Underneath it all, though, I longed to be loved and adored by somebody special.

I began to look at my body as the culprit. Negative thoughts about my figure began to haunt me as I began to see everything wrong with my appearance. Maybe the real reason I did not have many dates, I figured, was that I was not like other girls. My figure became an embarrassment, something I tried to hide with baggy clothes and long dresses.

Even the disappointments, though, began to shape my fantasy of what I really desired in a man. I resolved that I wanted someone who would treat me like a princess. More than that, though, he would be tall, dark and handsome—so handsome, in fact, that all the girls in my graduating class would be jealous. My fantasy man would sing tenor and play guitar to complement my alto voice and piano skills. My family would love him as much as he loved me.

In addition, on our wedding day, he would kneel like a knight in shining armor to kiss my hand before he kissed my lips. My high school best friend assured me that, *someday*, I would meet Mr. Right, and he would love me the way my heart so deeply desired. I clung to her words, for they nourished my soul.

My friend was correct. I did meet Mr. Right, just a month into college. Ironically, I met him about the same time I met all sorts of other great guys, and I made up for lost time going out on lots of fun dates. However, Kelly was the one who captured my heart.

Something about him set him apart from all the other men I was dating. The confusing thing for me, though, was that Kelly did not completely fit the picture of my dream man. My first thought about him was *cute* but not *handsome,* that all-important requirement. Furthermore, though Kelly was tall, he was not as tall as I had imagined. Even more puzzling to me, Kelly was clearly not my dream musician, since he could not hold a tune in the proverbial bucket. How could he be my Mr. Right if he could not sing?

Perhaps the most difficult piece of the puzzle to figure out was why, although they had seemed fine about my earlier boyfriends, my family did not care for Kelly at all. This hick from a dairy farm in Kentucky did not impress my family in the least.

Though some pieces of my fantasy just did not seem to fit, other things about Kelly were so much more and better than I ever could have imagined. He was good-looking like my kindergarten boyfriends; he was adventurous like my elementary sweetheart. He treated me with respect, the way a princess deserves. He accepted my physical standards (though, by this point, I must say that I was ready to lay those ideals down for him). Instead of wooing me past my boundaries, he chose to treat me and my body with honor.

Rather than going parking, we explored the area where we lived. Kelly took me out on wonderful dates when we were together, and he always kept his promise to write when we were apart. As the weeks of dating turned into months and the months turned into three years, I discovered that Kelly had become my Prince Charming.

We were similar in so many ways, and we were opposite in other ways that mattered. He *got* me, and I got him. In spite of some harsh doses of reality during our dating years, we were both smitten. A new fantasy, one that could actually become reality, had been created.

Kelly and Tosha Williams

Our Fantasy

After three years and three months of dating, it was time. The knight in shining armor drove up in his white car and swept his princess off her feet, taking her to the enchanted land where they would live happily ever after.

Our wedding day was a fairytale come true. Surrounded by sunbeams and flowers, family and friends, we exchanged our vows. My heart skipped a beat when my knight in shining armor kneeled to kiss my hand, just as I had always hoped he would. Then came the glorious moment when we were pronounced husband and wife. We enjoyed our wedding reception near "Swan Lake," a place that evokes romance in both fairytales and real life. A white, horse-drawn carriage later escorted us to our honeymoon suite.

Princesses live for the wedding day. Princes live for the honeymoon. April 24, 1993, was our fairytale come true. We had imagined it and fantasized about it; now we were experiencing it.

We had hoped, but we never could have dreamed it would be so good! Bygones were bygones, never to be bothered with again. Childhood fantasies, teenage fantasies, bad fantasies and misguided fantasies faded away. Now we were living *our* fantasy!

Our great fairytale had begun. We were destined to live happily ever after!

Your Fantasy

You have to admit, there is nothing like a good "happily ever after" story. Most relationships start here, and it is not a bad place to start. Fantasy is built, to some degree, on the hope that life has some possibility of utopia in it and that you *can* experience some "happily ever after."

Fantasy is the result of many things, and the fantasy you entered marriage with was certainly as shaped by your growing-up experiences as ours. We came into our relationship with fantasies that we reshaped as we dated. We married with a new fantasy that was not as much "his" or "hers" but "ours." We created a fantasy in the beginning of our relationship, and so did you.

Before we go on, stop to consider your story and your fantasy. These clues from your past have everything to do with the fantasy—and the reality—of your marriage today.

For Discussion:

Writing this chapter evoked many memories for us; some were wonderful while others were painful. Before we could continue with this book, we needed to stop, ask each other some hard questions and hear some difficult—and some, enjoyable!—answers. We encourage you to do the same. Here are some questions to get the two of you started:

1. Describe to your spouse what fantasy is according to the definitions used in this chapter and then according to how you perceive fantasy. Are the book definitions and your perceptions the same or different? How? Why?

2. What was your fantasy before you met your spouse? Trace the roots through your childhood, adolescence and young

adulthood. What expectations of romance, love and fantasy did you have when you met your spouse?

3. What early fantasies did you create as a couple, when you were dating and when you were beginning marriage?

4. Do you feel like your spouse "gets you"? On a scale of one to ten, how "known" by your spouse do you feel? Why?

5. Very few couples describe marriage as being a fairytale, although most would say once upon a time they hoped to experience that. Is this true of your marriage? We suggest that you begin describing what your fantasy is with your spouse in your marriage now. If your marriage could look like anything you want, what would it look like? What is "happily ever after" to you? Be honest!

2. the reality

"I keep asking myself, when is that moment in a marriage when a spoon becomes just a spoon?"
- Katie in The Story of Us

The town of Seaside, Florida, is an incredibly romantic place in the spring. Perfect sunrises to the east rival spectacular sunsets to the west. With balmy days, warm nights, peaceful beaches, cobblestone streets, rose-covered trellises and candlelit dining, Seaside has everything required for an appointment with fantasy.

Unfortunately, on our first night there, our fantasy collided with reality. We were angry at each other. Emotions flared, tempers heated and, before we knew it, we were close to a knock-down-drag-out. Instead of making love, we were making war, sitting on opposite sides of the bed disconnected from each other.

Certainly, there were some very normal reasons for this, including physical exhaustion from a couple of long travel days and emotional exhaustion from all that had just taken place in our lives. We were absolutely spent.

Those reasons aside, we really did not know why we were mad at each other. We just knew that, at the moment, our fantasy was being strangled by our reality, and we did not like it. We were in the perfect setting, but we were not experiencing perfection by any stretch of the imagination.

And we had only been married for forty-eight hours.

Our ideal of a perfect honeymoon had not included a fight on our first night in paradise. This was supposed to be the honeymoon of our dreams. As we both fumed, backs to each other, we wondered: what have we gotten ourselves into?

A New Phase: Fantasy Versus Reality

All we want is to live happily ever after. We want to be known. We want to be accepted. We want to be loved. We want to connect with someone else at a level that enables us to live out the most intimate fantasies of our lives. We want to experience and be experienced. That is pretty much why most of us got married.

Yet, here we are, caught in a paradox. The place where we most hope to experience REAL relationship is sometimes void of fantasy.

Truth is, every great fairytale has fantasy, but every great fairytale also leaves out a good dose of reality. Rest assured, marriage will not! Just as fantasy is part of your marriage relationship, reality will be as well.

We still want to live happily ever after. This desire has not diminished. Yet, in various ways, reality begins to affect our hopes and expectations, making us wonder if "happily ever after" is really possible. We personally have felt and pondered this in our own marriage. It seems to us that reality and fantasy go through a process in marriage. None of us plans this; it just happens.

The first phase of relationship is "Fantasy Apart From Reality," which could also be known as the "Happily Ever After" stage. Most relationships start in this pleasant phase. This was when you realized the person you were dating could be your soul mate. This was when you experienced the defining moment of realizing that you and this person could become an "us."

Sure, you may have stopped to consider the pros as well as the cons of the person you planned to marry. But, mostly, you saw the pros. When you thought about your fiancée or fiancé, you primarily considered what you would gain, not what you would lose. You did not walk down the aisle planning daily fights or anticipating consistent miscommunication. You did not eagerly hope for all the things that "in sickness" would entail. You did not overly focus on the problems in the relationship; you thought about how great it would be to be together forever. You did not think about the "what ifs"; you thought about the "what will be." Everyone begins here.

Relationship cannot be stagnant, though. It has a hard time staying in one phase; it tends to move on. So, then comes a new stage of relationship. Our official title for this next phase of a marriage relationship is "Fantasy Versus Reality." We jokingly refer to this stage as the "Shrek Takes a

Dump" phase. It is when the fantasies of your marriage collide with the smells of reality.

In the movie *Shrek II*, the blissful introduction comes to a screeching halt when Shrek marches into the outhouse and uses the pages of the fairytale book for a less-than-romantic purpose. Poor Princess Fiona knew she was marrying an ogre; she had overlooked his green-ness with the eyes of love. But this? The reality is that Shrek has some unpleasant sides about him that she cannot romanticize. So do all of us. Parts of reality just stink.

What is reality, anyway? Webster's Dictionary says that reality is, "the quality or state of being real," and "something that is neither derivative nor dependent but exists necessarily." Whew, lots of deep stuff here. Without having to ponder it like in college philosophy class, suffice it to say that reality just *is*.

Reality exists, whether you want it to or not. Out of necessity, reality imposes itself upon life, and, more pertinent to the topic at hand, reality imposes itself upon your marriage relationship. While fantasy is your creative way of staying deeply connected in your marriage, reality is, well, reality. Some of it is good and enjoyable; children are an example of a great reality. Some reality is painful and hard. (Children can be an example of this, too!) If it has not already, it is just a matter of time before your romantic fantasy collides with your reality.

In the "Fantasy Versus Reality" stage of a relationship, the passionate eyes, the butterflies in the stomach and the eager anticipation for one's beloved begin to—dare we say it?—lessen. Your passion does not go away entirely by any means.

Kelly and Tosha Williams

We are not saying you quit loving each other, and we certainly are not suggesting that your marriage is in trouble here.

It is just that, as fantasy and reality collide, the battle between selfishness and selflessness commences. Certainly, you may have experienced hints of this when you were dating, for life is never perfect. However, your battle intensifies once you get married, and it keeps getting more intense the longer you are married.

Gradually, reality begins pushing around fantasy. It is not a big deal at first because you can take some pain and still find a secret place in each other. A fight on the honeymoon leads two young lovers to enjoy the beauty of making up (and out!). A dinner date disrupted by your babysitter's desperate call is chalked up to the glories of parenthood. A miscommunication on the phone is blamed on a tough work schedule instead of a deeper conflict. A big fight about friends is assigned to stress rather than problems in your relationship. Any of these isolated from other pain is probably not going to destroy you. Your fantasies with your spouse can live on.

Unfortunately, reality just cannot leave fantasy alone. Reality begins shoving fantasy a little harder when your spouse becomes disappointing to you. Princess Fiona, relational as she is, discovers that her ogre wants to be left by himself. The Princess Bride realizes that her true love constantly saying, "As you wish," just does not fulfill her heart as it did when they fell in love. You begin to notice that your spouse is not as handsome or powerful or beautiful or creative as you had thought. A night out with friends is more agreeable to your spouse than a night at home with you. These are painful realities, for sure.

Your relationship is strong enough to handle these, but you are certainly not living in la-la land anymore.

Sometimes, the two—reality and fantasy—go to all out war. Your ideal of family relations is shattered by the downright meanness of your in-laws—and your spouse's lack of response. Your fantasy of a healthy wife is decimated, literally, by the surprising discovery of her anorexia. The pain of your spouse's physical issues destroys your dream of sexual fulfillment. Your hopes for a child become insatiable when the reality of infertility fills your medical chart. Painful reality stacked upon painful reality becomes too much of a heavyweight for fantasy.

In the "Fantasy Versus Reality" stage, you begin to realize, through a process of time and experience, that you have gained some things in marriage; but you have lost some things, as well. You gained security, but you lost freedom. You gained a companion, but you lost your individuality. You gained a partner, but you lost your exclusive control. You gained your dream, but you lost at least some of your fantasy.

Whether you consciously admitted it or not, you had hoped that your marriage would be a fairytale. Now you are beginning to discover that it is not. Inevitably, your relationship takes the hit for this.

The Unglamorous Opponent of Fantasy

For us on our honeymoon, our fantasy was perched precipitously on the edge of reality. Spending some time alone reading, journaling and doing what feeds our souls individually helped get us back on track together. The ocean breezes then quickly blew away the stench of reality, and the rest of our honeymoon returned to absolute fantasy.

However, there comes a point in every marriage when reality is not so easily forgiven and displaced by romance. It was not too many years into our marriage before the pressures of finances, bills, education, in-laws, mortgages, physical sickness and children took a toll on us—just as they take a toll on every couple we know. The stress gets high; the errors are not easily forgivable; the responsibilities are overwhelming.

This may happen in your first year of marriage; it may happen in your fifteenth year of marriage. Or it may happen somewhere in between. The *when* of this stage is different for every couple. Rest assured, though, that the *who* of this stage is the same for us all. *We all experience a time when our fantasy clearly differentiates from our reality.* Every relationship will have defining moments of pain when the hurtful realities of everyday life challenge the fantasy.

Then, there we are looking like deer in the headlights at what should have been obvious to us before our vows: the reality of marriage is not as glamorous as the fantasy of marriage. Reality seldom is. This realization *feels* like the sting of death, even though it is not necessarily deadly. "Fantasy Versus Reality" makes you stop and ponder about everything you have ever hoped and dreamed. It will force you to decide whether you want to be REAL in your relationship. This is actually a good thing, as we will see in coming chapters.

What painful realities oppose the fantasy in your marriage? The following is a list of potential "realities" you may be facing. This list is random, to give you the chance to process what is going on in your life. Your reality—to others—may be minor or extreme, but it is yours. Only you and your spouse truly know how painful your reality really is, so take into account *everything* that affects your marriage as you read this list.

Realities Opposing Your Fantasy:

- Educational or cultural differences
- Different expectations
- Pregnancy
- Children
- Work schedule, school schedule
- Drug or alcohol addiction
- Sexual addiction
- Pornography
- Depression
- Anxiety disorder
- Financial struggles
- Joblessness or poverty
- Family loyalties or ties
- Putting career ahead of marriage
- Unequal success between spouses
- Lack of freedom
- The right to do things "my" way
- Unfulfilled childhood dreams
- Unresolved ongoing arguments
- Career issues
- Resentment
- An affair
- Rape, incest or abuse
- The pace of life
- Infertility
- Sexual boredom, shame or dysfunction
- Selfish habits

Kelly and Tosha Williams

- Critical spirit
- Past sexual encounters
- Illnesses
- Death or illness of a child
- Emotional disconnection
- In-law conflicts
- Teen pregnancy of a child
- Obesity or eating disorders
- Personality quirks
- Emotional insensitivity
- Judgmental spirit
- Hygiene issues
- Blended family issues
- Spiritual differences
- War or military obligations
- Home renovation
- Continual relocation
- Friendships outside the marriage

Reviewing this list may bring up some of the pain you have been trying to avoid. There are the highest of heights to reach in marriage, but there are also depths to which we all plunge. Ideas will conflict with experiences; fantasy will conflict with reality. When hurt outweighs happy for a prolonged period of time, reality often gains the upper hand on fantasy. No matter how much you love your husband or wife, you find it difficult to engage that person on the same level as you did when reality was not quite so overwhelming.

What do you do when the pain of reality starts to hurt more than, or at least equal to, the pleasure of fantasy you share with your spouse? Maybe you are wrestling at this very moment with this question. Maybe you have been trying to figure it out for so long that you are almost at your wit's end. Perhaps you have only experienced a shadow of this issue in your relationship so far.

Or, maybe, you are reading right now thinking, *we will never let our reality take over our fantasy. That just won't happen to us. We will never let pain steal our passion. We will love each other as no one has ever before loved.* Do you feel this way? If so, then good for you! We felt that way, too, when we entered our "happily ever after." In fact, after getting through that first fight at Seaside, we felt like we were still on a honeymoon long after our first two-week vacation together.

The Story of Us

Alas, our seventh year of marriage arrived. Looking back, we are not for sure why that particular year was as hard as it was on our marriage. We had plenty of stressors, to be sure. We were leading a two-year old church, parenting a two-year-old child and expecting a baby. Finances were very tight, and Kelly's work schedule was quite demanding.

These realities should not have been able to harm our fantasy, but, that year, they did. In our seventh year, we felt the impact of "Fantasy Versus Reality" like never before. Reality gained the upper hand on our fantasy. We did not bounce back from the pain quite like we used to. We could not brush off the hurt and rekindle the romance as easily as we once did. Our relationship began to suffer.

During this painful time of our marriage, we found a movie that, to our surprise, we deeply identified with and from which we still draw insights. *The Story of Us* is a pointed movie about a couple (played by Michelle Pfeiffer and Bruce Willis) fighting for their marriage. You will see references to this movie throughout this book.

Like our relationship, Ben and Katie's marriage started out great, too. Ben recalls how pretty Katie was when he first saw her; Katie thinks of how unique Ben was. They fondly remember their dating relationship as well as the early years of their marriage and family.

Unfortunately, the happiness of their past is not enough to give them a happy present. In fact, the reality of their present is destroying the possibility of a happy future. Ben and Katie cannot enjoy fantasy together very long because they usually end up fighting again about reality. Though their past experiences were wonderful, their current experiences are just too painful.

For a time they work on their marriage by going to various marriage counselors. These sessions are helpful for about ten minutes, then reality starts bickering with fantasy again. Gradually, Ben and Katie learn to leave each other alone. Katie elaborates on their marriage this way:

> "I think the loudest silences are the ones filled with everything that's been said. Said wrong, said three hundred times...Until fighting becomes the condition rather than the exception. And, suddenly, without you even knowing it, it becomes the language of the relationship, and your only option is a silent retreat to neutral corners."

Ben and Katie's story differs from our story, yet we understand the emotions and feelings they express. In our seventh year, we were at the point of retreating into neutral corners. The honeymoon stage of "Fantasy Apart from Reality" was only a memory for us. We were experiencing the "Fantasy Versus Reality" stage, and it was beginning to take everything we had to keep the fantasy alive. Our reality was about to knock our fantasy down for the count.

We were a long way from the cobblestone, candlelit romance of our honeymoon. Instead of taking each other's breath away, the noxious fumes of painful realities were beginning to smother our marriage.

And it really stunk.

For Discussion:

In creating this chapter, we stopped to take the time to identify our painful realities. What is painful to us this year is, in some ways, different from what was painful to us last year. Yet some of our struggles are the same.

As you go through these questions individually then together, honesty is essential. Only as you identify the pain in your relationship will you be able to process it and communicate about it. The path to REAL relationship is carved, initially, with pain. Don't be intimidated, though. The path can lead somewhere that is healthy and wonderful.

1. Two phases of marriage have been described so far: "Fantasy Apart from Reality" and "Fantasy Versus Reality." Do you see your relationship in either of these? Which one? Why?

2. Of the painful realities we listed, which are parts of your life? How long have each of these been in your life? Or are

you wrestling with something else that is not on our list? What is it? How long has it been an issue?

3. Which of these realities have come into your life via your spouse?

4. In the battle of "Fantasy Versus Reality," which seems to have the upper hand in your marriage right now—fantasy or reality? Describe why.

5. Now, take some time to compare the lists you have each made about your painful realities. How do your lists differ; how are they the same?

6. How have your experiences in marriage differed from your imaginations of marriage? What realities are you facing that you never calculated into your fantasy? Are you resentful about this?

7. If you could create a new fantasy in your marriage right now, what would it be? Set the painful realities aside for a moment and talk together about your fantasies for your marriage.

3. the costs

"I never thought this would happen to us. I thought we were going to be the ones to go the distance."
- Katie in The Story of Us

We bet you never thought this would happen to you. You planned to go the distance with your beloved. When you embarked on the marriage voyage of your lifetime, you and your spouse saw stars rather than the clouds. You sailed off into the sunset making commitments to one another, proclaiming your ship unsinkable. Well-wishers waved you bon voyage for a happy, pain-free adventure. The band played, confetti fell, balloons floated and your journey began with bliss. Your own personal love boat was exciting and new.

Like the original Titanic, the fantasy of your Titanic was its beauty, uniqueness and mystique. In spite of that, somewhere along the way, things changed. Instead of sailing through the warm, tropical waters of fantasy, the Titanic of your relationship sailed into freezing cold waters. The skies darkened, the clouds became heavy and those soft silhouettes in the distance started looking more like icebergs than palm trees.

Instead of gazing lovingly into each other's eyes, you look fearfully at the danger all around you. You begin to realize that you had no clue, back when your voyage began, what you were committing yourself to. Reality introduces your fantasy to more than you ever imagined would be part of the relationship.

Rather than consumed by love, you are consumed by the impending pain. To your bewilderment, your romantic journey is becoming an unscripted, disastrous edition of *Survivor*. Your fantasy of marriage is on the brink of disaster.

You never thought this would happen. But, here you are experiencing what you were convinced you had avoided by the person you chose and the path you took to get here. Now, life is as you thought it would never be. Icebergs threaten the beauty of what you have shared. Reality has overtaken fantasy, and your passion, your love, and maybe even your marriage are threatened with sinking into the icy waters. You have just entered a new phase of your relationship.

We never thought this would happen to us, either. But it did.

Cold, Cold Waters

The first phase of relationship, "Fantasy Apart from Reality" (otherwise known as the "Happily Ever After" stage), is all about your dreams and desires for each other. Life is not pain-free, but it is blissful. In this honeymoon stage, all you see is how wonderful it is to be in love with one another.

During the next phase of relationship, "Fantasy Versus Reality," you discover that every fairytale has its unpleasant, even painful points. Just like Princess Fiona realizes that her prince has some unpleasant sides, you find out that your beloved is not as perfect as you had imagined. Your relationship goes through some adjustments, some less-than-enjoyable periods. You start experiencing painful realities. Overall, however, you still maintain your fantasy, hopes and dreams for your marriage.

Some of the painful realities become dangerous icebergs in the next phase, though. When your relationship comes up against realities harsh enough to harm the ship of your marriage, you have entered the "Fantasy Drowned by Reality" stage. We call this the "The Titanic Sinking" phase, when the iceberg of reality attempts to destroy the Titanic fantasy of your relationship.

Some relationships bounce back and forth between phases. A bad period of reality shoves fantasy away; a good day, week or year brings back the fantasy. However, when the dreams in your marriage have all but disappeared or when a let-up in the stress does not invite some romance back into your relationship, you are no longer fluctuating between phases. When you cannot find fantasy with your spouse anymore, you have officially entered this third phase of marriage.

Many relationships tread water in this phase for years. The "Fantasy Drowned by Reality" phase can be the slow drowning of a relationship with a few swimming moments of happiness until the waters of reality rise and drown out any fantasy that might have still been afloat in your hearts.

In this phase, conflict is the norm and positive communication is not. You and your spouse become adversaries at worst or dissatisfied roommates at best. When your love boat starts sinking, you begin to question whether your relationship can go the distance of the journey—and whether you even want it to. Your fantasy is drowning, but you hardly notice, because who *wants* to hold on to fantasy when you are not sure if you even like the person to whom you are married?

If you have not experienced this, just keep living. Every couple will have defining moments of pain when reality begins to drown their relationship. The iceberg you face in your marriage may be a sick child, a financial disaster, a terminal illness, an affair, a difficult in-law or any number of other painful scenarios.

Cold Waters

For Katie and Ben, in *The Story of Us*, the full reality of their iceberg occurs when they are getting a separation. As they are about to go their different ways, Ben looks over at Katie and poses the million dollar question:

> "Isn't this the moment that one of us is supposed to say, look, this is ridiculous—we love each other, all couples go through this, let's give it another try?"

If Katie would speak the word, their ship might sail away from the iceberg. Ben wants to figure out how to intertwine their fantasy and reality once again, but Katie's only response is silence. She is hurting too badly to respond any differently.

The two of us identify with this moment because we have been there in our own way. Despite our issues during the "Fantasy Versus Reality" stage, we survived the notorious seventh year of marriage that we discussed in the last chapter. The full reality of an iceberg appeared in our twelfth year of marriage, when we came into our own desperately cold waters of "Fantasy Drowned by Reality."

That year was one of the most physically, financially, spiritually and relationally challenging years of our lives. In a matter of six months, almost everything about our lifestyle changed, and our family's existence became, to some degree, a matter of survival.

At first we plunged gung-ho into the challenge. We felt like we were doing what we were supposed to do, so we turned our faces to the wind and pressed on. By Christmas, though, we could hardly take it anymore. Tosha was especially depleted; she was sick and her emotions were out of control. While she was not suicidal, the lack of life she felt breathed death into our marriage. And fantasy? We could hardly engage on that level.

We were not looking for this iceberg when we hit it. We knew we were in chilly waters, but somehow we missed the 'berg we were getting ready to hit head on.

You seldom start out looking for icebergs, but, in retrospect, they often seem as if they are looking for your Titanic. The historical Titanic could have sailed a different direction before it hit iceberg-laden waters, but your Titanic does not have a choice in navigating all obstacles. Reality brings pain, sometimes the self-inflicted kind, but just as often, the unasked for variety.

Then you find yourself almost in a state of shock, asking your spouse, *how do we get out of this?* Other than the freezing water lapping the sides of your ship, the only sound you hear is silence.

Reinforce the Ship

Hope is not lost, though. Whereas the historical Titanic was not prepared for disaster, the Titanic of your marriage can be. We want you to know there are some ways to sustain your marriage in the sinking moments. (If there were not, this book would not be worth writing—or reading!) Your marriage need not go down like the Titanic.

Anything worth fantasizing about for as long as you did regarding your future marriage is equally worth fighting for. You and your spouse have the power—if you both want it—to keep your ship from sinking.

Just saying vows at the wedding altar and being married are not sufficient, though. To keep the ship afloat, whether in freezing or balmy waters, you must live a REAL marriage.

You should know that this *will* cost you. It will not come easy. (Few things worthwhile about being an adult are easy, we might add.) But, REAL *is* worth experiencing, we have discovered. Remember, marriage is—or, at least *was*—the majestic Titanic of your romantic dreams.

When your Titanic hits the cold waters and the icebergs, you can, if you want, put on life preservers, go below deck and make repairs to the damage. Surviving in REAL mar-

Kelly and Tosha Williams

riage is not just about jumping on a lifeboat when times get tough. It is about strengthening the ship you are already on.

This is when you begin to *Realize the Cost* of REAL marriage. The cost of REAL is what you have to pay in order to be an "us" instead of a "me." It is what you choose to do to strengthen your ship instead of letting it sink.

Paying the cost of REAL marriage means you will have to conquer your fear and get away from the known to experience the unknown. Your Titanic may have not seen the icebergs yet. You may have just hit the icebergs or be almost completely submerged by them. Though going below deck may feel like an end, this is where your personal "story of us" begins the first chapter of REAL. The title of this new chapter is *Realize the Cost.* How do you do this?

A newly married couple we know of hit an iceberg when the young husband found out—in the hospital, no less—that his new bride struggled with a serious issue. Worried, scared and frustrated, the young man blurted out to his father-in-law, "I didn't sign up for this."

Tactfully, the father-in-law responded, "No, you may not have known you were signing up for *this,* but you *did* sign up the day you married my daughter."

So much truth is found in the insight of that father. Whatever you end up facing with your partner, the truth is that you signed up for it. You made a vow, which is easy to do when times are good. But when the tough times come, the waters get cold and the icebergs loom, the real test arrives. Will you stick with what you signed up for? You will, if you are willing to *Realize the Cost.*

Stay on the Ship

The first way to *Realize the Cost* in REAL marriage is to "Stay on the Ship." No matter the cost, no matter whether you thought you signed up for this particular struggle or not, you live out your vow by not giving up on your marriage. When the seas of life get rough, you do not jump ship. When the fantasy in your relationship is being drowned by the reality, you do not give up. You stay committed to your spouse and your marriage.

This is not a popular suggestion in our culture. Our culture could care less if you stay committed to your vows. Divorce carries little stigma. The motto of the day is "To your own self be true." Our society gives you the license to go outside your marriage to look for your fantasy, whether you find it in a person, computer or magazine rack. You do not have to "Stay on the Ship" to get what you want.

Nonetheless, whatever you choose, whether you are willing to stay on the ship of your marriage or not, you will have a cost to pay. The costs of not giving up, of being committed to your spouse regardless, may seem too high. It may seem too pricey to stay on the ship and rediscover fantasy with your spouse. However, the costs of letting your marriage fantasy drown are also very high. The costs of a failed marriage are staggering.

You get to make the choice. In this choice of the cost, you are not choosing *whether* you are going to pay the price, you are choosing what you are going to pay the price *for*. Everything in life costs something; everything worth having involves sacrifice. Is your marriage something—is your spouse someone—you are willing to pay the cost for?

You might say, "You don't know what I have to put up

Kelly and Tosha Williams

with." Certainly, you may have a very difficult person to live with. We are not saying that you can "make" your marriage entirely REAL if your spouse is not committed to the same thing. (Neither are we saying you should stay on the ship if you are being abused.)

Yet, in normal circumstances of pain and struggle, what do *you* choose? You cannot control your partner; you can only control you. Are you willing to stay committed to your marriage regardless?

We can tell you now, if you are hedging your bets or have ultimatums for your spouse, this will not work. To *Realize the Cost* in your marriage, you must first commit yourself to your spouse *regardless*. This may be easy to do right now, or it may be extremely difficult. The question is: are you willing?

If your answer is *no,* then the dissolution of your marriage—whether by law or by lifestyle—is not a matter of *if* but *when.* If your answer is *maybe—maybe I'll stay committed if he does, maybe I'll try again if she will change, maybe I'll stay in this marriage until the kids are grown*—then we sadly wish you good luck. Holding your heart at a distance will not keep it as safe as you might imagine.

Conversely, if you are someone who is willing to risk yourself for something greater than yourself; if you want to experience all that life has to offer with the person you said your vows to; if you want to keep the chapters you have written in your marriage and write new ones, then you are someone who is answering *yes. Yes, I am committed to my spouse, regardless. Yes, I will do what it takes to keep our marriage and fantasy afloat.*

When you make this decision, you are reiterating the vow you made on your wedding day: "This is who I am. I am your spouse until death do us part." These sacred words drip with promise and pain. These words are easy to say naively on your wedding day, long before you are bouncing off icebergs in the freezing water of reality.

However, these significant words are the first step toward REAL. We encourage you not to give up on your marriage. Take a risk, stay on the ship and commit yourself to your marriage no matter the cost.

Strengthen the Hull

The second step toward *Realizing the Cost* in REAL is to "Strengthen the Hull." In *Realizing the Cost*, you see the price you pay as not only expense but also an investment. This mindset is the difference between seeing your health insurance premium solely as an expense or seeing that same premium as a way to protect your family. The first expense brings grief to your wallet, but the latter investment brings some security to your future.

Realizing the Cost is not just about forging through the hard times and making yourself commit to a difficult marriage. *Realizing the Cost* is about continually endowing your relationship with a healthy future. Making regular investments along the way strengthens your REAL marriage so that it can sail a happy, if not pain-free, journey.

History shows us that those who built the Titanic were short-sighted in this way. Certainly, they built an amazing ship, one that they claimed was unsinkable. When the ship left port on her maiden voyage, she was filled with the best life had to offer.

Kelly and Tosha Williams

Unfortunately, she was not adequately prepared with what might have prevented—or at least lessened the impact of—disaster. Adequate lifeboats could have changed the history of that infamous ship. A disaster plan might have helped them stay afloat until help arrived. Avoiding iceberg-laden waters may have averted disaster altogether. Somebody—the owner, the builder, the ship's captain—was too caught up in the fantasy of the Titanic to prepare for trouble. Somebody did not continue to strengthen the ship.

You do not have to navigate your marriage this way. You can choose a different course. Once you commit to staying on the ship, you can choose to do the necessary work to make your marriage stronger and safer. Be aware, though. *Whenever you address realities that are painful, your relationship will initially hurt more.* Do not avoid this. Lean into it.

Maybe your ship left port without you and your spouse learning how to talk deeply. You can *Realize the Cost* in your marriage by working on new communication techniques. You may choose to spend the next six months intentionally focusing on this issue. There are wonderful books and conferences that can help you with this.

Perhaps you struggle with trusting one another. Do not keep sailing to the Bahamas with this issue in tow. Drop anchor and start strengthening the hull by figuring out the why's and the what's and maybe even the who's that are making you distrustful.

Maybe your marriage has already hit an iceberg and is beginning to feel the laps of cold water. You have chosen to work on your marriage by reading this book. Keep going! Another thing you can do is to send out an S.O.S. signal for help. Get accountability for your marriage or seek professional counseling. Every investment you grant your relationship can help keep it afloat another day so you can write more chapters in your story.

Maybe your marriage has not yet encountered the "Fantasy Drowned by Reality" stage. We want to encourage you that, no matter how good your relationship is, you can always make it better and stronger. Remember, they thought the Titanic was in great shape—until she hit the icebergs. Keep strengthening the hull of your relationship. Throughout the rest of this book, we will discuss more ways to strengthen your marriage. Some of these will be painful for you, but we encourage you that they are worth it.

When you *Realize the Cost* in REAL marriage, you commit to your spouse and do the work necessary to strengthen your marriage.

Bail Water

The next step in *Realizing the Cost* is to "Bail Water." There is no way to know, on your wedding day, how much it will cost to be married to the person you are walking down the aisle with. You cannot know today what costs will be required of you tomorrow. Sure, you may be able to guess the costs, but there is no way you can *know*. Although the Titanic's captain might have strengthened his ship better, there was truly no way he could have entirely foreseen the disaster awaiting his ship.

We might not know what awaits us in life, but we can boldly live the reality dealt us—and try to make it better. Of course, you could jump ship when reality gets too difficult.

Kelly and Tosha Williams

However, if you have decided to stay in this relationship, and if you are willing to strengthen the hull of your marriage, then start bailing water. Start making sacrifices for your spouse.

Reality is that your relationship will cost you. Loving your spouse every day will cost you. Maybe your spouse is sick or your sex life is not what you hoped. Maybe you grieve every day because the person you thought you married has turned out to be someone different. Maybe you have hit the iceberg of a wayward child or financial disaster. Remember that the costs of marriage, whether it is dismal or wonderful, are inevitable. Paying the price by loving your spouse *through* your reality is a part of REAL.

What does it cost you on a daily basis to face reality and bail water in your marriage? What are the sacrifices you make to propel *your* marriage toward REAL? What are the burdens you bear for your spouse? (We will discuss these in detail in chapter twelve.) In the process of writing this book, the two of us sat down one morning and talked about the buckets we each bail for the other. We discussed what our relationship costs us individually. Doing this, in this context, was not self-ish. It was our way of facing the reality of our relationship and seeing how we each keep our relationship from drowning.

For instance, our marriage has faced incredible in-law conflicts. This iceberg nearly destroyed us early in our marriage. Fortunately, Kelly learned to bail water by allowing Tosha to deal with her own family. Instead of trying to control the situation, he stepped back and entrusted Tosha. Tosha, on the other hand, began to bail water in this situation by learning how to put Kelly first in her loyalties. It is a fine balance to love one's birth family well while keeping your marriage the highest priority.

Another iceberg in our reality is finances. Like many people, we have an extremely tight budget, which can be a continual source of stress. Thankfully, each of us is learning how to bail water in this area. Kelly keeps a constant watch on the finances and runs our farm to bring in extra income. Tosha shops seven different grocery stores for sales to make our grocery budget stretch further.

Also, between pastoring a growing church and raising a large family, our schedule is extremely demanding. Neither of us gets much relief from dealing with these potential icebergs, and, indeed, we would not want to be free from them altogether. Nevertheless, we have had to learn how to bail water to keep our marriage afloat in these areas, too. Kelly limits what he is involved in outside of the immediate needs of Vanguard Church and our family so that he can be at home as much as possible. Tosha manages the majority of home responsibilities. She cares for the crying baby or sick children during the night so that Kelly can get the rest he needs to do the work of the church.

We each have our own bucket to bail, and we do the bailing in partnership for the sake of each other and our family. This is what love looks like. Love sacrifices for a REAL relationship. Wherever your ship is right now, look at the sacrifices you make to bail water for your spouse and marriage. These are the price that you pay to love your spouse well.

Kelly and Tosha Williams

Your Titanic Need Not Sink

The fantasy of your relationship may be sailing into some ominous waters. The Titanic known as your marriage may have hit a number of icebergs. Those around you, if they were in your boat, would have already jumped ship crying, "Every man for himself!" You might be thinking this yourself as you consider jumping into the chilly waters of divorce.

Before you jump, though—whether emotionally or literally—stop. You can always let this ship sink and jump on another one, thinking that journey will be a better experience. You can always get divorced and marry somebody else. You can always choose to live the rest of your life floating in your own personal lifeboat.

If you let the ship of your marriage sink, though, many chapters of your story will be lost. Not lost in the sense that they never existed, but lost in the sense that they will be unfinished. The pages of your story will be like an uncompleted manuscript, a lonely, depressing thing floating in the cold waters of reality.

Sure, there may be bad parts, but there are good parts, too. Your story is worth preserving. No matter what port you set sail from or how long you have been on this journey of *Realizing the Cost*, you can sail on.

If you are both willing, you can repair your marriage. Fantasy may be buried under the chilly waters of pain, disappointment or maybe even hatred, but you can restore its loveliness. The icebergs can cause an awful lot of damage, but they do not have to sink your marriage. Your marriage can survive if you are committed to stay on the ship, strengthen the hull and bail water when reality starts submerging you.

In the next chapter, we will talk more about investing in your marriage. Journey with us through the chilly waters of reality as we recapture and rebirth over time the fantasies of your heart for one another.

Your Titanic can sail again. Calmer waters beckon; new sights entice. Fantasy, adventures and new experiences await your marriage. Care to go there with your spouse?

For Discussion:

1. Everything in life costs something, and marriage is no exception. The cost of your relationship, whether it is dismal or REAL, is inevitable. The question you must answer, individually and as a couple, is whether you are willing to pay the price *for* your marriage. Where will you cash in your heart, your time and your life? This is something you must ponder personally.

2. So far, we have described three phases in marriage. The first is "Fantasy Apart from Reality," which is the honeymoon stage of relationship. The second phase is "Fantasy Versus Reality," when your "happily ever after" comes up against hard times. The third phase is "Fantasy Drowned by Reality," which is when the pain and problems of life destroy the hopes and dreams you share. In the next chapter, we will describe "Fantasy Meets Reality." Of these four phases, which best describes your marriage. Why? Do the two of you agree on where you perceive your marriage is?

3. We encourage you to go on a date and do the following exercise together:

4. Write down on a piece of paper what it costs you to be in relationship with your spouse. Think about the ways you have to bail water in your marriage; consider what you do to strengthen the hull of your family. Your list may include things like: regularly apologizing, staying committed to boundaries your spouse has requested or communicating in a certain way. What do you do to make your marriage good? Write this down.

5. Read this list to your spouse, starting with the words, "This is what it costs me to love you." When you are finished reading the list, affirm your spouse by saying, "This is what it costs me to love you, and I am willing to pay this price, because I do love you."

6. Give your spouse a turn to do the same.

7. Regardless of where your marriage is, you are not past the point of redemption if both of you want it. Do *you* want redemption? Does your spouse? If you can answer "yes," share your thoughts with one another. What is something the two of you can do today to strengthen the hull of your love boat? Do it!

4. the investment

*"I'm not talking about having every one of my needs met.
I'm talking about connection—a look,
something that says we're on the same side here."*
- *Ben in* The Story of Us

During our engagement, we decided that it would be helpful to our future marriage to take ballroom dancing lessons. Being broke college students, though, we did not go to a teacher in a professional dance instruction studio. Instead, we checked out a learn-to-dance video from the public library.

For several weeks, we scooted the coffee table out of the way in Kelly's little apartment and turned the VCR on in hopes of making our feet learn how to move together to the rhythm of the music. Unfortunately, coordinating our feet quickly proved too hard, too complicated and too time consuming for us. We could not seem to make our bodies go in the same direction, and we were rapidly getting very frustrated with one another. Rather than create a new reason for conflict, we finally decided to return the video and quit our dance endeavor.

We figured that we did not need to know how to ballroom dance to move well together. After all, we were already waltzing quite well to the music of love.

The Music of Relationship

When you are first together, you dance to the music in your hearts, whether you know the steps or not. There comes a time, though, when the music is not so easy to hear anymore. After we got married, there were days that the music stopped and we could not find a rhythm together to save our lives. When fantasy and reality collide, the intimacy of marriage can shatter.

Our music completely stopped one Christmas Eve morning, at a time when life is supposed to be the happiest. After months of pent-up frustration, hurt and anger, we had a huge blow-up. The explosion rocked our world and left us both deaf to all but pain. Just a short time later, Kelly had to leave for church to prepare to lead the annual Christmas Eve services. Tosha stayed home to finish holiday preparations and get the kids ready for the evening. We both felt like fools, having lost a very special day to anger and hurt.

Hours later, there we stood, side by side, in church, worshipping on a holy night. Tears streamed down our faces, not because, as some observers may have thought, the event was so sacred to us. We had tears because we knew the ugliness in our hearts. Our reality was painful, but even uglier than the pain was how we were treating each other. Taking out life's pain on each other was not getting us anywhere good. Instead, it was sending us to the bottom of a very cold ocean. Instead of feeling warm fuzzies on that holiday night, we were shivering from the chill of our relationship.

Our love boat hardly resembled the majestic Titanic of our dreams that had sailed out of port twelve years prior. On that awful Christmas Eve, when our marriage almost hit the bottom, we saw how ugly the bottom really was. This realization became a great turning point in our marriage. We did not know what it was going to take to sail to a better place; we did not know how to dance any new steps or even find a new song. We just knew that something had to change for the better between us.

Doing the Dance

Living a marriage that intertwines fantasy with reality is a delicate dance. Many things about "Fantasy Versus Reality" attempt to pull you off the dance floor and away from one another. Sometimes, life has a way of drowning the music of fantasy altogether.

Just as we abandoned our college dance lessons, many married couples give up on learning the steps of intertwining fantasy and reality. It is too much of a challenge. Coordinating your steps and learning a new dance is difficult, complicated and time-consuming. You know the names of couples who have decided that it is not worth the effort. They are the divorce statistics.

Yet, we believe that learning the delicate dance of intertwining fantasy and reality is worthwhile. When you determine to do this, you are choosing a new stage, which we call "Fantasy Meets Reality." This is a major step toward REAL. Even if you never get the steps quite right (and none of us get it perfect, by the way), the amazing thing is that, in the process, you are in each other's arms, hearing the rhythm of each other's hearts, swaying to life's music together.

Along the way, you begin to rediscover some of the music you heard back when you were dating, engaged or first married. Better yet, when you choose "Fantasy Meets Reality" for your marriage, you start to make new music. You begin to create new experiences for your relationship and to connect on new levels. (We will talk about ways to do this in the last section of the book.) The dance of your relationship becomes much more exciting.

However, learning a new dance is intimidating. Very few people enjoy getting out on a dance floor when they do not know what they are doing. It takes a brave soul to risk your ego and learn how to dance in a new direction. This requires an investment.

The first letter of REAL stands for *Realize the Cost*. Without a doubt, you have seen the cost as reality has set into your relationship. The cost of REAL is what we discussed in the last chapter: stay on the ship by committing to your spouse regardless, strengthen the hull by doing the work required for your marriage and bail water by facing reality and sacrificing for your spouse.

After you *Realize the Cost*, then comes the time to pay that cost with an investment. The investment will exact a price from you because nothing worth having comes free.

Intertwining fantasy and reality in marriage will require sacrifice—a sacrifice that may demand more of you than you have ever given before. This is where you suck it up and step out on the dance floor, regardless of who is watching, who can do it better or how inept you feel. You sacrifice your pride and risk a new dance for the sake of your partner, for the hope of your marriage.

The investment to *Realize the Cost* is learning the dance of vulnerability. This is challenging in every relationship.

Vulnerability initially feels about as awkward as getting out on a dance floor with a bunch of strangers, all of whom appear to know the macarena inside and out. Nonetheless, slowly but surely, vulnerability begins to intertwine your reality together with your fantasy in ways that you have yet to experience. Vulnerability begets vulnerability. Being vulnerable to your spouse can create a desire in him or her to be more vulnerable with you. When this happens, vulnerability leads to trust. The best of fantasy can happen in a marriage strengthened with trust.

Determined to Dance

You are never going to get to healthy fantasy in your marriage by just saying you want it, though. Healthy fantasy is not a name-it-claim-it endeavor. You cannot just say, "We're going to have a great love," then sit back and wait for that to happen. You cannot expect a romance that reaches the heights, weathers the storms and survives the fires without doing something to give it that strength. You cannot have a passionate relationship that lasts for a lifetime unless you pay the price for it.

Whatever your hopes and dreams, goals and desires for your marriage are, they will not come true apart from sacrifice. *Whatever way you define the best of fantasy in your relationship, it comes with the price tag of vulnerability.*

The problem is that vulnerability is as difficult as it is uncomfortable. How do you become vulnerable to your spouse? Just spilling the beans about your past or your desires is probably not the best way to go about it. Simply putting on new lingerie or trying something different sexually is not the core of vulnerability. Even handing over your journal, which contains your most intimate thoughts, is not necessarily the most effective way to begin being vulnerable.

These may be ways to be vulnerable, but the heartbeat of vulnerability is deeper than that. We have three specific steps for you to begin working on. These are not easy, we know. We are continually trying to move together in this delicate dance. Initially, these steps feel a million miles away from fantasy.

Reality works on behalf of fantasy here, though, because as you invest in the reality of being vulnerable, you will feel your relationship begin to dance toward new fantasy. We believe you will find that so, so worthwhile.

Learning the Dance, Step One: Be Honest about Your Own Selfishness

This is where it all begins. The first step of vulnerability is to be honest about your own selfishness. If you want to intertwine fantasy and reality in your marriage, then you must be

Kelly and Tosha Williams

honest about *you*. Not your spouse and all his issues or her problems. You must focus on the reality of yourself.

It is much easier to focus on your partner's need for change instead of your own. Pinpointing your spouse's selfishness is not usually a problem. Just yesterday in our marriage, I let Kelly have it for the way he was handling our family's evening schedule. Going running after a crazy day at work was his priority. I felt hurt and angry that he did not see my need for a break and make that his priority, too.

In retrospect, Kelly may or may not have been selfish in how he chose to handle the evening. The thing is, in hindsight, I see that *I* was selfish. Sure, I was exhausted; I justifiably wanted a break. So, when Kelly did not immediately respond to my needs exactly as I wanted, I put him in the box of "you're selfish." I wanted my needs met and my expectations fulfilled. I could not have cared less at that moment about focusing on him; I focused on me.

More often than not, I focus on my needs instead of Kelly's. Situations like last night force me to look at, wrestle with and admit all the sludge in my own heart. I prefer to blame all, or at least most, of the ugliness on Kelly. It is a lot easier to focus on what he does wrong than to see what I do wrong in our marriage. I would rather focus on changing him than changing me. That is the selfish truth.

Investing in REAL marriage requires honesty. I am a selfish person; you are a selfish person. We all are. Denying you are selfish—or making your selfishness relative to the greater selfishness of your spouse—is not going to help matters, either. Being honest about your own selfishness is one of the best ways you can strengthen your marriage.

In *The Story of Us,* Ben admits his selfishness to Katie. Earlier in the movie, she had yelled at him, "Not for one second have you seen it through my eyes." When Ben realizes the ugly truth of this, he goes to find Katie. As soon as she answers the door, he bursts out with this admission:

> "I wanted to know what your high was today... My high today was about you. Tonight I saw myself through your eyes... and I'm sorry."

I am sorry. Three words that make all the difference in the world. Three words that we all need to say. All of us are selfish, especially with our spouses. Some marriages have more selfishness involved than other marriages, but do not miss the point: every marriage partner is selfish to some degree.

You may say, "You just don't know my husband," or "You can't imagine how selfish my wife is." Yes, you may have an extremely challenging partner. It is not about comparing yourself to your spouse right now, though. As you read this section, try to look at yourself through your spouse's eyes. How are *you* selfish? Don't justify or give all your reasons right now. Just be honest about yourself. This is how you begin to become radically vulnerable.

For example, instead of listing the ways your husband is selfish, make a list of the ways *you* are selfish. In what ways do you put your needs over your wife's needs? How do you elevate your desires over your husband's desires? In what ways do you do your own thing without being accountable to your wife about it? How do you *force* your husband to validate you or feed your soul? How are you unwilling to meet your wife's needs?

Once you have thought about and realized the ways you are selfish, you must go one more step. Realization of how you have been selfish is not enough. You must confess it to your spouse, communicate a desire to change and create a plan for change. Honest confession creates an environment where the music can begin to play once again.

I could simply ignore how I treated Kelly last night, but that would not bring anything good into our relationship. Just saying "I'm sorry" would be nice, but this would not bring true healing. In order to be vulnerable and really speak love to Kelly, I need to say something like, "Sometimes I am so selfish, and last night was a case in point. I am sorry for hurting you. Will you forgive me?" After saying this, I must communicate to Kelly how I want to work on talking to him instead of blowing up at him. (This, of course, is much easier to write about than to do.)

Easy or not, vulnerability like this lays a foundation for healthy fantasy in REAL marriage. *You* focusing on changing *you* feels more like love than control to your spouse. Control always stifles fantasy. When you focus on changing you, your spouse will feel love and have a reason to trust you, because you are not just trying to change that person, you are seeking to change yourself.

The two of you share a powerful story. You focusing on changing you is an investment in that story. As we will see, this sacrifice will lead to fantasy you have yet to experience in your marriage.

Dance Step Number Two:
Let Your Spouse Be Honest about Your Selfishness

When you watch *Dancing with the Stars*, it is obvious that, most of the time, the dance steps get harder before they get easier. A contestant who was thrilled with her first achievement sits down and cries because her new routine feels impossible.

It is the same way with this second dance step. Even though it is hard to focus on your own selfishness and confess it to your spouse, it is going to be even harder to learn what is next. It may even feel impossible. Nevertheless, the fantasy of dancing in the stars with your spouse is possible only through continuing the steps of vulnerability.

If you want to intertwine fantasy and reality in your marriage, you must not only be honest about your own selfishness, you must also allow your spouse to be honest about your selfishness. You must look in the mirror your spouse holds up for you.

This will be downright painful. Everything in you will revolt against it. You do not want to hear about what you do wrong; you feel hurt and condemned enough already. Honesty such as this is easier to avoid than pursue.

For the sake of REAL marriage, however, you must allow your spouse to speak *to* you *about* you, and you must listen.

Now, there is definitely a time and a place to do this. When you are in the heat of a fight or when you are surrounded by friends or kids or even complete strangers, you are not in a good setting to take this step. You need to wait until both of you are calm and as rationale as possible. Privacy is a must, whether that is in an intimate booth at a restaurant or the quiet of your bed-

Kelly and Tosha Williams

room. Once the setting and emotions are conducive, you should start talking to each other. And start listening.

Don't be defensive; don't initially agree or disagree; don't offer excuses or justifications. Let go of your pride and listen to what your spouse has to say. REAL is not real until you listen and internalize your impact on the person you are trying to be REAL with.

Not until you are willing to see how your selfishness impacts your spouse will you become truly vulnerable. When you smell the stench of your own selfishness and swallow the pride of your own defensiveness, this is when you begin to feel the REAL relationship.

You will want to run away, defend yourself, argue, clam up, throw in the towel or assume it is not supposed to be this way. However, if you hang in there and listen, you are on the path to REAL. This is good stuff. Why? Because when you let your spouse speak into your life, you begin to make the investment of vulnerability in your marriage. This vulnerability will lead to greater trust, which will, in turn, lead to the healthy fantasy you have dreamed of.

In our relationship, when we go out on a date, we do not initially try to make it a perfect evening just because it is a rare opportunity and needs to be special. We have learned not to act under the illusion that everything in our relationship is perfect.

Instead, we often go for a drive or to a quiet restaurant. Sometimes we take our journals because it is easier to read our written thoughts than to articulate them fresh. Other times, the feelings and honesty are so close to our hearts that just a few sentences start a deeply needed conversation. In the quiet of moments like these, we engage each other in honesty and vulnerability.

Tosha must listen to what Kelly says about her life, and Kelly must listen to what Tosha speaks about his life. Even in the best of settings, we do not always do this perfectly in our relationship. Pride rises up, and so does the desire to be defensive. Sometimes the honesty spills out in the midst of an argument, over the phone or around the children. We do not always get the method right, and our reality becomes more painful as a result.

Then again, when we do the delicate dance of vulnerability well, when we share honestly about each other in a private, loving setting, it is amazing how much more fantasy we experience later. Learning layers of your spouse in the context of reality makes the fantasy all the better. The investment you make in your marriage by being vulnerable and honest about your selfishness has great rewards.

It does not stop here, though. After focusing on your own selfishness and letting your spouse speak into your life, there is one more step toward intertwining fantasy and reality in your marriage.

Dance Step Number Three:
Seek New Fantasy within Your Reality

Good news! As far as we are concerned, you have done the hard part in learning steps one and two. Being honest about yourself and allowing your spouse to be honest about you are tough steps to learn and dance. When both of you focus on your own selfishness and allow honest dialogue about your struggles, you open the door to new trust in your marriage. Your reality will never be the same.

Now you can build upon that vulnerability. Few people will enter fantasy in a marriage if they do not feel safe there. Nonetheless, vulnerability in the communication aspects of your marriage can help you feel safe in the fantasy aspects of your marriage. A wife who feels like her husband has heard her heart is much more likely to try a new sexual position. A husband who can articulate how he does not like being controlled by his wife is much more likely to do the dishes. *Fantasy does not just come out of nowhere in a REAL marriage; it is the by-product of trust and vulnerability.*

Vulnerability affects everything about the fantasy in your relationship, no matter what reality you are facing. In order to intertwine fantasy and reality in your marriage, you vulnerably live them, both of them, together, all along the way. Your fantasy and reality become two sides of the same coin.

In REAL marriage, neither fantasy nor reality takes the place of the other, but both exist simultaneously in your hearts. At any given moment in any given day, your REAL marriage can experience both of them. As this happens, you begin to discover that your fantasy can become more powerful because of your reality.

We remember how this took place in our lives when we brought our first child home from the hospital. We were so happy with our new baby girl. Our new family of three was a dream come true for us.

The reality, though, was that Tosha was already exhausted and overwhelmed with caring for an infant who seemed to scream constantly. She had entered motherhood somewhat naïve to the physical demands. She quickly discovered this tiny person would demand every ounce of her strength.

On the other hand, I felt like I had lost my wife, because I was lonely and felt second-place to our new creation. My feelings may have been selfish, but they hurt anyway. I remember rolling over in bed and saying to myself, "What have I done?" We had been so close; we had done everything together as a couple up to this point.

Coping with our new reality in the separate corners of our lives, we both had the sneaky suspicion that things would never be the same between us. Our lives had changed forever.

In this situation, vulnerability meant honestly talking through the pangs of our new reality and figuring out how to adapt to them. In the midst of being new parents, we had to create new ways to connect to one another.

Life brings change, does it not? Good realities and painful realities force us to adapt, whether we want to or not. The question is, when change comes, do you fight the reality because you want your former fantasy to remain intact? Or do you allow your fantasy and reality to adjust together?

Whether your current reality is a new baby, a new home, a new job, a sickness or struggle, a bunch of kids or no kids, things will never be the way they were. Life marches on, bringing some adjustments that you may choose (like expanding your family) and others that were your worst nightmare (like sickness or financial ruin). You can fight against the changes and keep wishing in vain that things would go back to the way they used to be. Or you can forge ahead into creating a new fantasy with your spouse.

As you do this, your fantasy and reality will intertwine

Kelly and Tosha Williams

with one another. Believe it or not, your fantasy can become even more powerful because of your reality.

After thirty years of marriage, one woman said to us about her husband, "I do love him more and deeper. Who would have guessed that would have happened after all these years?" Through the good times and the bad, this couple figured out how to make each other matter and fall more and more in love.

How does this happen? How can fantasy become more powerful because of reality? Instead of overpowering reality or being drowned by reality, how can fantasy *meet* reality in your marriage?

Fantasy can become more powerful because of reality for one reason: reality costs you something. Your vulnerability in your relationship is the result of sacrifice. The trust you share has cost you something.

Because of this, when your fantasy meets your reality, you have a deeper appreciation for the person you are engaging in your fantasy. Your spouse, the one you experience the highs and lows and mundane of reality with, is also the one with whom you can experience the highs (and, sometimes, lows) of fantasy.

Toward the end of *The Story of Us*, Katie comprehends the truth of this in their marriage. In an emotional plea to Ben, she talks about the dance they share. Tearfully she expresses the realization that is bubbling up from within her heart:

> "We're an us. There's a history here, and histories don't happen overnight. You know, in Mesopotamia

or ancient Troy or somewhere back there, there are cities built on top of other cities.

"But I don't want to build another city; I like this city. I know…what kind of mood you're in when you wake up by which eyebrow is higher, and you always know that I'm a little quiet in the morning and compensate accordingly. That's a dance you perfect over time. And it's hard, much harder than I thought it would be, but there's more good than bad, and you don't just give up … "

In the end, Katie got it right. Leaning into your commitment to stay on the ship can lead to greater fantasy along the way. You journey through it all together, and the journey is richer because you understand the price each of you pays to make it all work.

You also realize that your spouse is not with you because you meet all her expectations or his needs. Because of reality, and sometimes in spite of reality, your spouse chooses to stay with you. That commitment to a common reality is where the music of fantasy can begin to play.

The Story of Us

After that emotionally devastating Christmas Eve, we set forth into a new year with the icebergs still clanging about our ship. The waters were still frigid, and the hull was still leaking. Our past investments were wonderful and set us up for the possibility of success, but these did not *ensure* future success in our relationship. New investments were required in order to keep our Titanic from going beneath the chilly waters. We

Kelly and Tosha Williams

needed a new strategy in order to awaken the music again in our marriage, so we began to search for a new rhythm.

Just a few weeks later, on our sixteenth dating anniversary, we began working on the concepts of this book. The journey we have experienced through this will affect our marriage forever. We are beginning to understand that, though our current reality may not become easier any time soon, our marriage fantasy can become whatever we want to make it.

We are beginning to see that our fantasy is a secret, safe place, a refuge for the two of us. Nobody else and nothing else can invade this space unless we allow it. The rest of our world might be exploding from stress, sickness and instability, but our fantasy is a place of solitude and peace.

Sure, there are kids banging on the door, bills waiting to be paid, decisions pressing to be made and responsibilities wrestling for our attention. Certainly, the fantasy looks different now than it did when we were one, five, seven or nine years into marriage.

Nevertheless, the refuge of our fantasy can still be found in the midst of our reality. When we do the delicate dance of fantasy and reality, we are more united as a couple.

As we experience our fantasy meeting our reality, we are finding hope for our relationship and joy we never knew could be experienced this far into marriage. We are not going to let our Titanic sink. There is still music waiting to be heard in our relationship. There is more fantasy than we had imagined could still exist waiting for us as we approach more wedding anniversaries.

To seek new heights of fantasy with your spouse, you must get past a quitting attitude. Certainly, you *can* quit, according to our legal system. You *can* quit by shutting down your heart to your spouse and refusing to be vulnerable. However, if you ever want to experience REAL, you do not quit just because you do not like things about your spouse or your marriage. Instead of quitting—or secretly wanting to quit—you lean in to your spouse for the whole story—the good and the bad, the wonderful and the difficult.

When you believe the story you and your spouse share is worth it, you get on the dance floor and learn the steps of vulnerability whether you are comfortable or not. You *Realize the Cost* and pay it. You make the sacrifice by investing in your marriage. You face reality while you dream fantasy.

Your personal "story of us" has a beautiful fantasy lingering in the midst of your reality. Step out on the dance floor and let the music play.

For Discussion:

As you seek to intertwine reality and fantasy in your marriage, we encourage each of you to look at your own life. Do not be afraid of what you might see. Our feeble attempts to reach outside our selfishness and pride are always awkward at first.

1. Think about your own failures, inadequacies, weaknesses and selfishness in marriage. Take an honest inventory of *you*. Write down what you realize about yourself.

2. After you have completed the first question, plan a date with your spouse. During that time, start a conversation with these words, "I've been thinking about who I really am, and I want to talk to you about how I've realized I

Kelly and Tosha Williams

hurt you." In this conversation, focus on the pain you have caused your spouse instead of the pain that person has caused you.

3. You should not just talk about everything you have done wrong, though. Take your vulnerability a step further. Let down your guard and ask for forgiveness. (Don't be surprised if your spouse is shocked!)

4. Articulate how you intend to work on these areas of your life. Start with the words, "This is how I want to work on these issues..."

5. Now let your spouse speak into the selfishness of your life. Open the dialogue with this mindset and these words: "I am committed to being married to you, and I want to be the best spouse you could ever have. So, I want to give you the opportunity to tell me how I've hurt you in order that I can know how to be a better person for you."

6. The dance of marriage is most beautiful when you move through questions two through five together. If the two of you are able to do this, breathe a prayer of thanks that you are married to a person who is willing to be vulnerable with you!

7. Now comes the fun part. Once you and your spouse have spent time answering the prior questions, then discuss the following. What fantasy would you like to experience in your relationship in the midst of your current reality? What do you each hope for at this point in your relationship? How can you begin to achieve these goals and fantasies in your marriage today?

Section Two:

Embrace Spiritual Guideposts

5. the path

"Two paths diverged in a wood and I—I took the one less traveled by, and that has made all the difference."
- Robert Frost

To the casual observer, our wedding was not much different than any other normal southern wedding. In fact, it was rather typical, with flowers and photography, bridesmaids and groomsmen, a preacher and musicians. As creative as we tried to be in planning our big day, it was pretty much just like everybody else's wedding day.

Except for one thing.

When the minister said, "You may now kiss your bride," a hush fell. Some, who knew us well, had anticipated this big moment. Others had noticed their bulletins said, "First Kiss," and they looked at us with curiosity. Still others, like meandering hotel guests, may have leaned into the atrium just a little further to see what was about to happen. Our wedding may have been normal up to this point, but it was not normal any longer. You see, the two of us were about to experience something we had never before experienced together: our first kiss.

Yep, you read right. Our first kiss. Before this day, our lips had never touched. Yet, there we were, in front of scores of people, getting ready to try out our first kiss. No back-seat parking or closet smooching for us! Nope. In front of an audience of about 250 people plus onlookers from the busy hotel, we kissed on the lips for the very first time.

It sure did not come off like most first kisses in the movies. In fact, it was one of the more awkward moments of our lives! As Kelly leaned in to kiss Tosha, she nervously leaned away. We about fell over in the process, and the audience erupted with laughter.

When we ultimately both leaned in the right direction—*toward* each other—we immediately became pros at what is so foundational in every romantic relationship: the kiss. The connection between two people that speaks what words cannot.

With this kiss, we began our married lives together.

Taking a Path

Having our first kiss on our wedding day was not an accident. We did not just put this off until April 24, 1993, because we figured it was not worth experiencing. We had not accidentally forgotten to show each other how much we loved each other before this. We deliberately chose to walk a certain path, and our decisions along the way affected our big day and our lives.

That was true of our wedding ceremony, and it is true of every marriage. Whether you consciously realize it or not, your marriage is where it is today because of choices and decisions you and your spouse have made along the way. Neither a great marriage nor a difficult relationship happens by accident. You do not "just happen" to arrive at this destination. You and your spouse have chosen paths that affect you today.

Granted, life has unexpected detours that put every marriage on side streets at times. Unfortunately, there will always be issues about which you must struggle *with* your spouse. Yet, if you are struggling *against* your spouse in your marriage, it is probably not because you all the sudden awoke one day and did not like him or her. Little decisions and big decisions along the way brought you to where you are today in your relationship.

This is what we want to explore in this chapter. Every marriage has arrived at the point it is via a path. That path is your story. The road you have taken is the storyline of your book. To understand why you are where you are, you must stop and look at the roads you have chosen up to today.

If you get a group of couples together to share their stories, you will hear as many paths as you hear nuances to each path. Every path has its good and bad, its easy and hard. Indeed, many paths beckon. You may have followed various paths at different points in your relationship, such as the path you took when you were dating, the one you chose when you were first married and the path you are currently walking.

In this chapter, we want to focus on the first paths of

relationship. Indulge us by letting us share with you our path. Our journey may seem very strange to you, but this road has gotten us somewhere that we believe is worth being and telling you about: REAL.

As we tell you about our story, we challenge you to think about the greater, more pertinent story: yours. Which path did you take when you were dating? Our dating relationship took place in the nineties; yours may have ended when you got married last year. No matter how long ago it was that you dated, we invite you to remember your path.

Our Path

In 1989, when we were eighteen years old, we left for college with dreams in our hearts and luggage in our hands. Neither of us could have imagined we were soon to meet our future spouse.

Within weeks, a heated class discussion prompted our first conversation. Ironically, that night's topic was, "Is there one and only one person God has for you to marry?" In hindsight, such a topic for our first conversation was prophetic. At the time, our casual words were only a follow-up to a discussion in which our personal viewpoints departed from those of the class and the professor.

Except for seeing each other in various classes that first semester, we had little interaction. Then one day, at the beginning of our second semester of college, Kelly asked Tosha out on a date.

When I called Tosha that first time, all I heard on the other end of the line was a garbled *"It's him!"* as she told her roommates that I was on the phone. She must have thought I could not hear her reaction, for she returned to our conversation very composed with a polite "Yes, I'd enjoy going out with you on Friday night." That was the beginning of our path.

Our first date took us both by surprise. I found that Tosha was more than just another pretty face. She was caring and compassionate, and she had a confidence that inspired and intimidated me all at the same time. I had never dated a girl who looked me square in the eye and told me what she was going to do with her life. I thought she was amazing.

Evidently, we both felt the same way about each other because I had never been on a better date, either. I discovered that Kelly was a gentleman and a dreamer. He had vision for his life, a passion and a purpose. We talked about our lives and spiritual things, and we even prayed together. Best of all, I found that Kelly liked dessert as much as I did! I had always hoped for a date like this, and I was so excited to see what the future held.

The future came to an abrupt end, though. Our date provoked excitement in both of us, but it also invoked something else in Kelly. My conversation with Tosha inspired me to dream, but it also heightened my insecurities. This made me look for reasons why I should not like Tosha. (By the way, if you look hard enough, you will find things not to like about everybody.) I made a list of what I did not like about her and convinced myself she was not the girl for me, because she was too much of this and not enough of that. Shortly after that first date, I pushed her away and ended the relationship.

When Kelly told me, in so many words, to "take a hike," I was devastated. Our first date had been wonderful, yet he was not interested in pursuing anything more. Unwilling for him to have the satisfaction of seeing my pride hurt, I told him that I agreed: we *were* too young for a deep relationship, after all. Then I turned and walked out the door.

Little did he know that I cried all the way back to my dorm room. As excited as I had been days before, I was now broken. I thought we had potential together, but he just wanted to be left alone.

When Tosha walked away, I was relieved at first, but that emotion quickly escaped me. The feeling of being smothered by relationship with Tosha was gone, but so was the inspiration from being around her. The way she honored my request to leave me alone heightened my desire for her. Though I hardly even knew Tosha, all I felt now was the emptiness from being away from her. It was just a matter of time before I called and asked her out again.

When Kelly invited me to the Valentine's Banquet, how could I refuse? I guessed he could not get over me, try as he might. This date, like the first, was wonderful.

From that point, our paths converged into a very regular, though curious, dating relationship. Unlike other couples who spent every possible moment together, we spent time together only about once a week. Once a week we would go out on a date, talk about what made us tick and get to know one another a little better. Our relationship became a steady flow of weekend dates, walks in the park, drives down the interstate and conversations about life. Something was happening in each of our hearts that neither of us had ever experienced.

Your Path

Hopefully, reading the story of how we started dating will remind you of how you and your spouse started dating. When did you meet? How old were you when you met, and where were you? How did you each respond to the other? Did you immediately start dating, or did you flirt with friendship for a while? Did anybody speak into your life about this relationship, or were you on your own?

Perhaps you have not thought about the details of your journey for a while. Now is a great time to reflect. Go out on a special date with your spouse for the specific purpose of walking down memory lane. Reflect, laugh and remember those first days of your relationship, when you initially began to learn about each other. The path you took back then begins the storyline of your book. Your story is part of who you are as a couple. Do not skip a detail, even if some of those details are painful.

Our Boundaries

Roommates and friends who watched our relationship often asked us about it. They wanted to know what we did on our dates and if we had kissed *yet*. When we told them how we spent our hours together, they just did not understand why we were not getting all mushy parking up somewhere in the mountains. Even at a Christian college, the general expectation for a date is to do more than go out to eat, take a drive and talk. We did not choose that path, though.

We did not even hold hands until, after four months of dating, Kelly asked me if he could hold my hand, and I said yes. Whether you are measuring by today's standards or those of the nineties, this was most definitely *not* a big deal. Still, for us, it was everything. Our hands touched, and this was the beginning of our physical relationship.

After five months of dating, we went to my home in Virginia Beach—"the place for lovers," as its advertising slogan goes. As the warm summer breezes blew off the ocean waters, we walked along the beach and our conversation came around to our physical relationship. We knew by now that we really liked each other, but we did not want impulse to destroy what we had begun to experience. As the ocean water tickled our toes, Kelly guided our discussion about the next step of our physical relationship.

I told Tosha that, back in high school, I had experienced physical relationships with other girls. But I had never had with them what I had with Tosha even without a physical relationship. I did not want to mess that up and suggested we wait until after the summer to choose the next step of our journey. She agreed.

When we returned to college for our sophomore year, our discussion returned to whether we would kiss on the lips. One momentous evening, we decided to stay on the path we had begun and see where it led us. We vowed that we would not kiss until we got married, should that day ever come. We made this pledge to each other, but, even more importantly, we made this vow to our Creator. Raising a vow to this standard was both frightening and awe-inspiring for us, for although a pledge between two people might be broken, a vow before the Divine is a fearful thing to break.

Having chosen the course for our relationship, the next

year of dating became a happy blur of enjoyable dates and intense conversations, long drives and adventurous hikes. We had tons of fun dating.

We did not kiss. We did not have sex. But we did learn to communicate and share every ounce of emotion with one another. And, surprise, surprise, we became friends, best friends, along the way. We were learning that it does not always take physical touch to communicate love and care. In fact, during dating we realized that it is easier to learn how to communicate *without* being sidetracked by physical intimacy. It seemed that we were onto something special.

This path gave us the opportunity to feel the insecurities of our relationship without trying to mask them with physical pleasure. Boundaries forced us to be REAL (though we did not know exactly what that was at this point).

Your Boundaries

We realize that our "no kissing" story may sound odd. However, that is the beginning of our physical story. It has everything to do with our relationship now, just as how you began your physical relationship has everything to do with your relationship today. Do not bypass the significance of this.

Good or bad, happy or painful, we encourage you to remember how you engaged physically when you were dating. All of your decisions, whims and choices along the way set the stage for where you are today in your relationship. Have you ever talked about this as a couple? Have you ever taken the time to stop and consider the impact these things from your past have on your relationship in the present?

Your physical relationship from back then has everything to do with your physical relationship now. We are not just asking you to jog your memory about your past; we are encouraging you to take a long, hard look at it as a couple. As you will see in chapters to come, the reality of your past totally affects the reality of your present, no matter whether it was positive or negative.

Think about questions like the following: How did you and your spouse interact physically when you were dating? When was your first kiss? Did you have sex when you first started dating? Did you wait until later in your relationship to have intercourse? Did you touch each other or take off each other's clothes? Did you decide to live together? What path did you choose sexually when you were dating? What boundaries did you establish or follow? Why or why not?

Your answers to these questions are the pages of your story. You do not want to rip these pages out of your book any more than you want to glorify them. They are what they are, and they are part of what makes you who you are as a couple today. We encourage you to share these pages of your story with each other and recount your perspectives of them.

Our Obstacles

After dating for a year and a half, we began to realize that our relationship had a future and talked seriously about getting married. One evening near the end of our sophomore year, we meandered to a nearby mountaintop called "The Bald Spot." Under starry skies, we sought direction from our Creator for our relationship, and we posed our question in

Kelly and Tosha Williams

a unique way. "If we should get married, let us see a falling star," we prayed, just to see what would happen. We lay back in the grass, looked up and immediately saw several falling stars. For us, this spectacular sign showed that our relationship was meant to be.

Soon thereafter, Kelly purchased a beautiful engagement ring that had a sparkling diamond set off by two small rubies. Our hopes were high and dreams were big. The world was ours, and we would someday be committed to each other for a lifetime. We were on cloud nine—until Kelly went to Kentucky and I went to Virginia Beach for the summer.

Quickly, that cloud became a storm cloud unloading torrents of rain and lightning bolts into our lives. Without explanation, my parents told me to end my relationship with Kelly. They did not give good reasons; they just gave a decree to quit dating Kelly, quit talking to him on the phone and quit writing him.

I was devastated. I could not understand why my parents would force me to kill a relationship that was so important to me. Granted, there are times when parents need to step in and rescue their child from a bad relationship, a relationship that friends and family alike agree is harmful to the child. My relationship with Kelly was not like that, though. Everybody—friends, teachers, leaders—who knew us as a couple affirmed that we had something unique. Everybody, that is, except my parents.

As a twenty-year-old, I intensely wrestled with whether to obey their authority. I could rebel and do my own thing, or I could submit to my parents. Finally, I decided to do the latter. I reasoned that if, amongst many other things, our

Creator could make stars fall for Kelly and I, then He could also work out the details of our relationship. I determined to trust Him no matter what happened.

With a broken heart, I picked up the phone and did the hardest thing I had ever done before: I told Kelly that our relationship was over. With those words, our dreams and hopes shattered. As high as our mountaintop experience had been before the summer began, this unexpected blow was now a horrible low. We still remember how much it hurt.

Not able to do anything to ease Kelly's pain, I spent the rest of the summer trying to forget mine. I tried to rationalize that what we had was not unique. I tried to convince myself that I did not really love Kelly.

While Tosha was agonizing in Virginia, I was wrestling with my own pain in Kentucky. I was angry, confused, isolated and insecure all at the same time. I tried to talk Tosha out of breaking up, yet she asked me to submit to her parents with her. So I did. Submitting to authority was a huge test for our relationship.

What I discovered that summer was something I had never before experienced. Even though it hurt, I chose to love Tosha, knowing I could expect nothing in return. This was new for me, and there was no well-trodden path to follow. I did not like it, but I did find something freeing in it.

As the summer progressed, I worked on the dairy farm to earn money to pay for a ring that no longer held the promise we had dreamed of, to pay for a ring intended for a girl who was no longer mine. That was hard, but it never crossed my mind to return the ring to the store. That diamond and ruby ring was Tosha's, regardless of what happened in our relationship. I realized that, no matter what, I would always love her.

When that long, lonely summer was finally over, we came back to college for our junior year. The first thing we did was go to a fast-food restaurant for a much needed face-to-face conversation. Because communication was so deeply imbedded in our relationship, we could not just start ignoring each other. We had to find some sort of closure.

Though I expected Kelly to be very angry with me, he was not. He responded to me, the person who had hurt him the most, in overwhelming kindness. "The ring will be yours someday," he said. "If it is not an engagement ring, then it will be a friendship ring, a reminder of what we've shared." Kelly's words brought tears to my eyes, humbling and honoring me simultaneously.

That year, our relationship went down a new path. We did not ask for this path, but it was the one delegated to us by our authority and ultimately, we believed, by our Creator. Like the ancient story in the Bible where God told Abraham to sacrifice his relationship with his son Isaac, we believed that we were to sacrifice our relationship.

Ashes to the wind, we knew that if our relationship was ever restored to us, it would be a miracle. For now, we had to let it go.

Your Obstacles

If you dated any length of time before you got married, you faced obstacles, too. You may not have been twenty with a decision to submit to your parents, but you certainly had some sort of issues to face. What road blocks did your relationship encounter? What unexpected problems blew up in your faces?

It may be painful to remember, just as writing this has brought back painful memories for us. Yet, this is part of your story, too. It is worth remembering because it is part of your path that brought you to where you are today.

Give yourself some props. If you are reading this chapter as a *married* couple, then you made it past some big obstacles! These obstacles that you faced and overcame together are a huge part of what gives your relationship value today. This part of your reality can make your fantasy even more promising because your reality cost you something.

Our Friendship

After dealing the deathblow to our relationship, I tried to forget about Kelly and began dating other guys. Kelly kept being my friend, though. Several times a week, he escorted me back to my dorm after my midnight shift at the campus television station. Other than that, we hardly ever saw each other. Kelly helped me without any requirements of reciprocation; he just cared. Friendship like that is valuable beyond description. Being responded to with kindness rather than anger was a gift.

Then, unexpectedly, Kelly called one night to tell me that he had been to the doctor several times about a severe eye problem. We had spent so little time together that I did not even know he had been sick. Kelly told me that some tests had come back and that the initial diagnosis was either lupus or bone cancer.

With this news, the stakes suddenly became higher. I hung up the phone and cried until I could cry no more.

Suddenly the realization hit: I had lost my relationship with Kelly, and now I could very possibly lose Kelly himself. As painful as it was to lose our relationship, the thought of losing *him* as a person was even more painful. No longer could I convince myself that he was not special to me. Kelly was more than just a great guy whom I had dated; he was an intricate part of my life.

That made me *know* that I loved him. My parents could terminate our relationship; serious health issues could take Kelly's life. Nothing can end real love, though. Even while life shattered around Kelly and me in many ways that semester, our love kept growing. This, we each knew, was the real stuff, the stuff on which you can bank a lifetime of promise.

In the following weeks, to the doctors' surprise and our delight, Kelly's follow-up medical tests came back negative. No one could explain what happened. Yet, without a doubt, Kelly was healed. He called to tell me the good news. We celebrated, albeit not together.

Just before Christmas break of our junior year, Kelly and I asked my parents if the four of us could talk about our relationship. They agreed. We nervously shared with them that we had honored their request not to date. For seven months we had barely communicated. During the fall semester we rarely saw one another. Nonetheless, our love had not dwindled but had, in fact, grown.

We asked permission to get married and, to our surprise, my parents granted it. Our relationship had come back from ashes. We were thrilled.

With the miraculous return of both our relationship and Kelly's health, we felt the world was ours once again. We were back on the path of creating our own "story of us." Life was good, and we exulted in our relationship.

During the spring semester, though, tragedy took our relationship down yet another road when a drunk driver killed Kelly's mother. I was extremely close to my mother, and the finality of her death was beyond words. If you have ever lost somebody really close to you, then you know what I am describing. My mother's absence from my life was a huge vacuum, a hole that would never be filled. Her death destroyed my heart, and it began a time of mourning in our relationship.

Just before I lost my mother, though, I regained this precious relationship with Tosha. Somehow, in the midst of the grief, I had to learn to trust Tosha even more as somebody who loved me, believed in me and cared for me. That semester, we would go parking, not to kiss and make out, but so I could lay my head in her lap and, in privacy, wail with grief for hours.

We did not ask for this path; the Creator gave it to us. The pain and grief was indescribable, yet it forged between us new vulnerability and strength in our friendship. Our communication deepened; our trust widened.

Within this dark period of deep pain, we had a bright spot. On a sunny spring day in our nation's capital, I finally slipped that diamond and ruby engagement ring on Tosha's finger. We promised each other that we would continue this journey together and someday become husband and wife.

The high highs and the low lows did not make our engagement perfect, though. We still had plenty of conflict to learn how to work through. So we found a book called *Fit to be Tied* by Lynn and Bill Hybels, the founders of Willow Creek Community Church. Every Thursday morning before English class, we went to breakfast at a local grocery store deli (which was cheap and surprisingly private) and discussed the chapters of this book. After all our relationship had gone through, this book gave us much to consider.

Away from the eyes at campus, we went at it, nothing held back. We were serious about REAL relationship, and we were going to do everything we could to have it. That final semester of college, we simultaneously finished our studies and completed our pre-marital training for REAL. Then we parted ways until we could be together forever.

Your Friendship

What happened in your relationship that made you know that your friendship was more than "just" a friendship? How did you realize that you were really in love with the person you married? As you approached marriage, the two of you had to learn to care for one another and support each other. What circumstances forced you to choose to lean *in* to each other rather than away from each other?

Your answers to these questions are priceless pages of your story. Reflect on them; write them down.

Our Love

As Tosha and I approached our wedding, I recall a few specific things about those final months before marriage. I remember counting the days until our wedding, discovering our honeymoon destination and anticipating having sex for the first time. Let me tell you, I was hungry for love. We both were.

Just because we had not kissed did not mean we were not passionate for each other. Quite the opposite was true. The vow to purity in our physical intimacy only made the desire greater. Our wedding would be a reunion after months apart and a fulfillment of three years of desire.

Finally, our wedding day arrived. In a beautiful hotel atrium, we pledged our lives to one another. Our wedding day was a day of wishes and dreams fulfilled. We said our vows, and then we experienced our first kiss. It was crazy, embarrassing and wonderful all at the same time.

Hours later, on our wedding night, we discovered one another like never before in our lives. We had saved ourselves for each other, and now we gave ourselves to one another. Sure, we were novices at physical love, but that did not bother us. Our honeymoon was for discovery and practice, and it was bliss.

This was the beginning of a new chapter in our lives.

Your Story

That is the story of the path we took up to marriage. It is a path based on some ancient guideposts, which we will see in the next chapter. You may see your relationship reflected in our path, or you may see that your path was nothing like ours. You may like the path we took, or you may be struggling to see why on earth anyone would ever choose to go that way.

Regardless of what you think about our story, what is your story? The reason we write so much of our history is to make you think about the nuances of your own story. Each one is important and worth remembering. What made the two of you become friends? How did your love grow and develop?

Before you go on, take the time to write out your path that led you to marriage. Make a date with your spouse to write your story. Go to a coffee shop with your laptop. Find a private place with some paper and pens. Whatever way you do it, be honest about your path—the good, the bad and everything in between.

Your dating, engagement and wedding day stories are as unique as ours. Don't forget the details. This is *your* "story of us."

For Discussion:

We have asked you many questions throughout this chapter, and we have included some of these in the following list. Plan a night out with your spouse to answer and discuss these questions.

1. What was your first meeting like? How and where did you meet?

2. When did you begin dating? Can you recall together some of the minute details of that first outing? Have fun remembering them! How could you possibly re-create this date and re-live it again?

3. When did your physical relationship begin? What did you do together? Why or why not?

4. What pain and problems became obstacles for your relationship? How did you work together to overcome these?

5. As the text said, if you look hard enough, you will find things that you do not like about everybody. By now, you certainly know what you do not like about your spouse. What do you do about this? Is there something that *can* be done about this? How are you treating your spouse because of this? Have you been vulnerable about this? Spouse, are you willing to change what can be changed?

6. Were the two of you friends before you married? What are the things that made your friendship strong? What made you know that your friendship was more than a friendship?

7. When did you *know* you had fallen in love with your partner? *What* made you know that you loved this person? Who was the first to realize that *this* was love? Who was the first to articulate it?

8. What path led you to engagement and, ultimately, marriage?

Kelly and Tosha Williams

6. the guideposts

"This is what the Lord says, 'Stop at the crossroads and look around. Ask for the old, godly way, and walk in it. Travel its path, and you will find rest for your souls.'"
                                        –from the book of Jeremiah 16:16

At first, we did not notice the "dead end" sign. It was not until well after we had packed everything we owned, purchased the property and moved our family there that we noticed it. You would think we would have seen the big, imposing yellow sign posted at the beginning of our street. However, we did not notice it. Our eyes were too enamored with our dream property at the street's end.

We had received an e-mail from a friend telling us about a property for sale. He briefly described the place, then urged us to go look at it just for kicks.

We were not looking to move at the time, but, on a whim,

we drove over to see the property. By the next day, we had made an offer on it. Within three months, there we were, beginning our lives at our "dream property." And now, here we are.

In our family's opinion, this place abounds with wonder. Trees, a creek, fields and meadows, wildlife and birds—this place has it all. In the summer, wildflowers adorn the long driveway, and, in the winter, freshly fallen snow glows in the moonlight. Our new home really is our dream come true.

Our new house, on the other hand, is not. This fixer-upper has required much more work than initially visible. We have re-done literally every square inch of the house, from the support beams in the crawl space to the wiring in the ceiling. The results of our effort are increasingly worthwhile, but we have about killed ourselves in the process. There have been days, weeks and even months when we would like to go back to our old home. Life was much easier there.

If we had just observed the road sign—that guidepost that screams "dead end"—we might have saved ourselves a lot of grief, or we might have at least been better prepared for what we were getting ourselves into. Noticing the road sign probably would not have changed the outcome of our decision to buy the property. Sure, some days have been so hard that we would gladly go back to our old home. Nevertheless, *most* days we would do it all over again in a heartbeat because this "dead end" has become our home.

We chose our home because we believed it was the perfect place for our family. We chose it because we were enamored with its ideals. We believed all the work would be worth it, because this is our dream property. We were in love with what *could* be and what *would* be. How could we not choose this?

Kelly and Tosha Williams

The Signs We Miss

Funny thing how once you make a person or place a permanent part of your life you start noticing all the things you did not see before. Things you do not like, things you wish were different. Now every time we turn down the path to our home, we see the "dead end" sign. It bothers us, but we cannot change it unless we want to move. Covertly, we might take down the sign, but that would not change the fact that our "dream property" will always be located at a dead end.

It may seem a stretch, but, really, it is the same way with relationship. The guideposts speak truth about where you are, even if you did not observe those guideposts originally.

No man chooses his wife because she has a "dead end" sign hanging around her neck. No woman picks her husband based on the negative signs she sees when dating him. In our culture, you choose your spouse because that person is your "dream girl" or "dream guy." This person made you happy, fulfilled your hopes, brought out the best in you and helped you reach new goals.

You chose a path to marriage with your dream person because you believed it would lead to your fantasy marital relationship. The path you chose was the one that you believed would bring you to the best chances of success.

Whatever course you took to marriage, though, it was marked with guideposts to help you. These signs speak truth about life, relationship and marriage. Maybe you and your spouse followed these guideposts in your relationship. On the other hand, perhaps you were so focused on your dream person that you avoided the road signs trying to direct you along the way to marriage. Or maybe you arrived at the wedding altar without even seeing the guideposts, just as we arrived at the real estate closing without seeing the "dead end" sign.

Whichever route by which you came to marriage, one thing is for sure. Although you may not have seen the guideposts before you said your vows and closed the deal, you eventually will see or feel the need for them. Guaranteed.

The Ancient Path

So here you are. You said your vows to the person of your dreams. You promised to love your spouse, for better, for worse, in sickness and in health "until death do us part." You invested your hopes and dreams in this person believing you found your soul mate. Now what?

In the first section of this book, we discussed the "R" of REAL—*Realize the Cost*. Each of you must choose to pay the price, whatever it is, if you are going to experience the REAL marriage you were created for and desire to have. As you *Realize the Cost* and choose to pay it, you invest in your spouse. That is how "Fantasy Meets Reality" begins.

Now, in this section of the book, we invite you to consider the "E" of REAL relationship: *Embrace Spiritual Guideposts*. In our worldview, we believe that the Ancient Scriptures, also called the Bible, give many spiritual guideposts for REAL marriage. We believe that God created marriage and that, since He created it, He knows the way to experience it best. The Bible offers God's map for marriage; the verses of the Bible are God's guideposts along the way. We call this way "The Ancient Path," and it leads to REAL marriage.

This may not be your worldview, and we respect that. We

Kelly and Tosha Williams

are not asking you to buy into our spiritual worldview; we are simply inviting you to let us share with you the guideposts from the path we have chosen. From the beginning, these guideposts have dictated how we walk in relationship with each other.

Both the guideposts and our story are counter-cultural. We are quite aware that what we are writing is so strange and unpopular that it is fodder for late-night talk show hosts who have nothing else to joke about. Yet, we believe that these guideposts have guided our relationship down a path toward REAL.

In your relationship, you may never have known these guideposts existed or you may have intentionally followed them. Or you may have chosen to ignore the guideposts when you were establishing your relationship. Regardless of your past, if you want a marriage that is powerful and passionate and lasts for a lifetime, then read on. Your past relationship is what it is. We encourage you to consider the Ancient Path, not as condemnation, but as guideposts that can help you in the *now* of your relationship. You may need to re-adjust your course based on the guideposts to help you get on the right road. Or you may need to re-walk a few roads down memory lane in order to deal with the ramifications of bad paths chosen.

These guideposts from the Ancient Scriptures can lead your marriage relationship down a new path that will not dead end but will direct you toward REAL.

Guidepost Number One:
You are made for more than sex.

This guidepost teaches that there is more to life than sex and marriage. Ultimately, you are made for experiencing your Creator's presence. Still, along the way, He cares about your body and your sexuality. The Ancient Scriptures tell us:

> You can't say that our bodies were made for sexual immorality. They were made for the Lord, and the Lord cares about our bodies.
>
> 1 Corinthians 6:13b

Nothing sexy about this one. It is not very provocative and probably seems just a bit strange. Right now, you may be rolling your eyes and getting ready to pitch this book. Hold on, though. Stick with us just a little longer before you give up on REAL.

There is a Story behind your story, and it is this: you are more than a physical being. You were made for more than the love of humans and animals. You were made for more than marriage. You were made for more than sex.

Certainly, sex and love and connection are huge parts of being human. Ultimately, though, you are a spiritual being. You were made to feel the love of your Creator through experiencing His presence inside of you. The deepest vacuum of your heart can be filled only by the One who made it.

The path of the ancient guideposts starts here. Your body was created with a purpose and that purpose is to experience your Creator. This being true, you must not let your sexuality hinder your purpose. What you make as your supreme focus in life will determine the extent you feel and experience the Creator of your soul.

It is easy enough to make a relationship with another human being your supreme focus. Having sex meets your immediate needs and feels good. Your soul will still be lonely and unsatisfied, though, unless you also experience the supreme reason for your existence: having a relationship with your Creator.

Why not just have sex? For this reason: hidden within the deepest parts of your heart are uncharted territories with divine expectations. These are part of the greater Story of your life. You may not even be aware that these expectations are supernatural or that only the Creator can fulfill them. No human will ever fully meet your needs; only your Creator will. When you try to fill your voids with a person and sexuality, eventually your relationship will deteriorate because neither of you has anything left to offer the other.

If you can learn early in your relationship that no person will ever be entirely enough, you have a chance to experience REAL marriage. Furthermore, if you give yourself pause to consider your Creator, you will find that He deeply cares about you. The Ancient Scriptures teach that He even cares about the marriage you have and the sex you experience. All the other guideposts are built upon this foundation. God is not some enemy in the sky trying to kill your fun. He is the ultimate romantic who wants you to experience His best for your life.

Our Story

The decisions we made in our dating relationship—and

that we make in our marriage now—are based on this first guidepost. We embrace the fact that we are spiritual beings and that we have a greater connection to each other through spirituality. The ultimate reason for our REAL relationship is to connect, not just to each other, but to the One who created us. Our story is about more than us. There is a Story behind our story.

That we are married today is, really, a miracle. We had thrown our relationship like ashes to the wind, not knowing whether the pieces could ever again be found. When our relationship was restored to us, we knew that God did it. But here's the thing. Even if He had not done so, even if He had not given us the desire of our hearts, we believed back then and still believe that He cares about us. The Ancient Scriptures show that God is concerned about our human relationships, but He is even more concerned about our relationship with Him. He is the Story behind our story.

What did this look like for Kelly and I? Well, for example, when my parents ended my relationship with him, I submitted to them because, ultimately, I trusted God as the Author of my life's story. I believed that if God truly cared about me, as He says in the Ancient Scriptures that He does, then He would care about this part of my life, too. Believing that He had my best interests—and Kelly's—in mind made me more capable of following my parents' authority regardless of the outcome. As I now read this part of our story in retrospect, I can see that God was intentionally writing pages in all our stories that we could scarcely understand at the time.

Redeeming Your Story

There is a Story behind your story, too. No matter how you experienced sexuality outside the context of marriage, there is a great deal of hope for the future chapters of your life. God wants a relationship with you. You may or may not want it right now, but it is available to you as long as you live.

Stop right now and ask God to reveal Himself to you in a new way today. We are certain that He will answer your prayer. We encourage you to develop your relationship with the Creator, no matter where you are in your spiritual journey. At the end of this book, we will describe how to do that more in depth.

Still, whether you embrace a relationship with the Creator or not, the guideposts He designed can still lead you to REAL marriage if you will follow them.

Guidepost Number Two:
You will yearn for sexuality before its proper time.

This guidepost teaches that you are going to want to experience sexuality, but that you should not engage in it, before its proper time. Over and over in the book of Song of Songs, the lovers desire physical experiences, yet they wait until the time is right. Scriptures say this:

> One night as I lay in bed, I yearned for my lover. I yearned for him, but he did not come…Promise me…not to awaken love until the time is right.
>
> Song of Songs 3:1, 5

Sexuality is not something that—ta-da—you all the sudden start wanting when you finish your education, get a good-paying job, sign a mortgage on a new home and stand with your future spouse at the wedding altar. Nope. Thirteen-year-olds long to be touched when they are barely out of elementary school. Sixteen-year-olds enjoy sex on prom night, long before they are ready for real love. Twenty-year-olds want intimacy even if they do not end up getting married until they are twenty-nine. Whether you are ready to get married or not, you are usually ready to experience sexuality once you enter puberty.

Why did the Creator make our bodies this way? We do not know for sure, but we do know this: sexual yearnings before marriage are beautiful and powerful. These longings feel amazing, and they create in us intense desire for another person.

The desire for sexuality before marriage creates a depth of intensity that the Creator wants to grow. He wants our sexual yearnings to deepen through time and sacrifice. He wants us to have great sex—in proper time.

Many couples in our society give in to sexual passions all too soon and, without even knowing it, ruin the immediate chance to learn something apart from sexual activity. Loving someone, feeling that love to the core of your being, yet refraining from the sexual expression of that love creates self-control.

Big deal! Who wants self-control when you can have sexual fulfillment? Believe it or not, at some point in your marriage, you may have strong sexual desire for someone else other than your spouse. Controlling your passions with your future spouse will help you control your passions when you

Kelly and Tosha Williams

are passionate about someone other than your spouse. Think this will never happen to you? Chances are, it will.

The sexual self-control you learn before marriage through not satisfying the yearnings of your sexuality is actually a gift to your spouse. Self-control gives you a much better chance in marriage of staying faithful to one another.

Our Story

When I was a teenage girl in high school, an older married woman told me that what you allow yourself to experience prior to marriage is not nearly as exciting or enjoyable after marriage. The experiences you save are the experiences you savor.

Of course, this could not mean that if you have sex before marriage then you will never have great sex once you get married. Nonetheless, my friend's words always made me ponder as a single. What enjoyment might I lessen in my future marriage if I engaged in something outside of marriage?

As a young person, I was naïve to life. Yet, I did want to someday experience a great love; a marriage that could go the distance; a passionate relationship that would last for a lifetime.

So, I made a commitment not to kiss until I got married. I was determined to save this simple but profound intimacy for the man I would spend my life with. Despite opportunities to kiss and ridicule by peers when I did not, I kept my pledge through my teenage years.

This commitment totally affected Kelly and I when we dated. It is part of the reason we decided not to kiss until our wedding day. Of course, the more our relationship developed, the more we yearned to experience intimacy together.

If we were going to wait to awaken sexual love, though, then we had to have self-control. If we were not going to kiss, we were probably not going further down the road of having sex, either. To say it bluntly, putting off arousal enabled us to put off climax until we were married and the time was right.

Redeeming Your Story

Not every couple chooses the route we did. Statistics show that *most* do not. Whatever path you chose, the guideposts speak to that part of your story.

Looking back, when did your body begin to long for sexuality? Certainly, by the time you were dating your future spouse and engaged to that person, you were feeling the desire for passion. Did you indulge in it? Did you allow yourself to experience it? Did you wait?

It is good to stop and consider how this has affected your marriage. Do you have a hard time engaging one another sexually? Is your sexuality uninhibited? Are you able to control your passions now, or do you struggle with them?

If you are a Christian and you chose not to follow the Scriptures in your relationship, have you ever stopped to mourn and repent for this? It may seem like all this is just stuff from the past, but really, it has everything to do with your present. Maybe today you need to say to your Creator, *I am sorry.* I am sorry for ignoring this guidepost before I got married. Maybe you need to say to your spouse, *I am sorry.* I am sorry for my selfishness in our dating relationship. Maybe you need to confess and repent as a couple. Do this today; don't let shame and regret haunt your marriage.

Kelly and Tosha Williams

The best part of the guideposts is that the Creator always offers redemption. *Always.* The Creator is in the business of taking the broken parts of our lives and healing them, for our good and His glory. What parts of your story are just waiting for redemption? Do not let another anniversary pass before you and your spouse ask the Creator to redeem this chapter of your life.

Guidepost Number Three:
You will suffer if you ignore sexual limits.

This guidepost teaches that if you ignore sexual limits, you create baggage for your future marriage. Consider these words from Ancient Scriptures:

> Run from sexual sin! No other sin so clearly affects the body as this one does. For sexual immorality is a sin against your own body.
>
> 1 Corinthians 6:18

In our society, as long as consenting adults are involved, anything goes. Pornography, X-rated television and three-somes are acceptable ways to find pleasure. When you are dating, you get it on just for fun. When you are married and sex is not so fun anymore, you bring in a third party to spice up things.

These may feel great for a time, but your body cannot forever withstand sexual experiences that go against the guideposts. The Ancient Scriptures teach that sexual sins will harm you. Just as a car engine is designed to run with oil, your body was made to run with sexual limits. When you violate these limits, your body, your soul and your mind suffer.

Maybe you already know what we are talking about because you have already experienced the pain we are describing.

The only way to keep from violating your body sexually is to stay within the limits and establish boundaries. We know…that seems so traditional, even archaic to today's relationships. Waiting to have sex with the person you are dating seems, well, crazy—especially if you are going to get married anyway. After all, you have to make sure you are sexually compatible.

Moreover, if you are married, isn't it occasionally helpful to try something new—like multiple partners? Maybe pornography will help you engage your wife better. Perhaps a secret romance will get it "out of your system." This is the way our society processes relationships; this is most definitely not the way the Creator of relationship designed us to live in relationship.

The sexual limits the Ancient Scriptures establish are sexual abstinence before marriage and monogamous purity during marriage. Contrary to popular opinion, not just anything goes. Third parties are not okay, whether they appear in your marriage in flesh and blood or via a screen or paper. Sex outside of marriage is not okay, no matter how much you want to have sex before marriage or how unfulfilling sex may be in marriage.

If you ignore these sexual limits, you will create baggage for your marriage. Whether you experience sexual sin prior to saying your vows or after you are married, you are filling your emotional, physical and spiritual luggage with a great deal of pain.

On the other hand, if you follow sexual limits, you will lay a strong foundation for your marriage. This will not make

Kelly and Tosha Williams

your marriage perfect, but it will give you a great chance for REAL. It will give you the opportunity for your fantasy to meet your reality.

Our Story

In the four months leading up to our spring wedding, we saw each other only two times for what amounted to mere hours. It was probably good that our visits were brief because, after three years of dating, we really struggled to maintain our purity. *Really, what's the point in not having sex when you are planning to get married anyway? Let's just go ahead and show each other how much we love one another!* Our rationalization exponentially increased as desire and passion did.

We remember the drowsy winter afternoon when we were right at the point of violating the sexual limits. After so long dating and being so close to marriage, we were hot for each other. We knew we could have sex if we wanted to, but we also knew that if we waited, then the yearning would only purify and grow the passions we had for each other. We chose to pay attention to the sexual limits established by Scripture. For a few more months, verbal communication would have to suffice until we could indulge ourselves.

Setting sexual limits prior to marriage—and helping each other live within them—laid a strong foundation for our future marriage, a foundation with benefits we are still experiencing. For all the times before marriage when we wondered if sexual purity really matters, we have heard the answer "yes" resound more loudly with every passing anniversary.

Redeeming Your Story

Of course, it feels good to have sex. That's why people have sex! Sex feels awesome but, outside monogamous, committed marriage, it eventually will not feel so good. We believe that you cannot prove the Ancient Scriptures wrong on this one! Sex outside of marriage brings hurt, frustration, emptiness, betrayal or distrust into your relationship. Even that "perfect" shining moment some people have does not feel too good when it becomes an untouchable fantasy never again to be experienced.

It is impossible to avoid the suffering that comes from sexuality experienced outside of marriage. Your body was not made for sexual immorality, and it will suffer because of it.

Have you ignored or violated sexual limits somewhere along the way? We encourage you to go down memory lane and re-visit your sexual past. We live in a society where it is okay to experiment sexually. Did you give this a whirl in your past? Are you playing with this in your present? What sexual experiences have you had outside the bounds of a monogamous marriage?

The guideposts tell us that these will eventually destroy you. However, the Creator wants to redeem you and heal you. He waits for you to come to Him about these pages of your life. Are you willing to be vulnerable about this with Him?

Guidepost Number Four:
You experience healthy sexuality only in marriage.

This guidepost teaches that if you want to have healthy sex, get married! The Ancient Scriptures say this:

> ... Yes, it is good to live a celibate life. But because
> there is so much sexual immorality, each man should
> have his own wife, and each woman should have her
> own husband ... If they can't control themselves, they
> should go ahead and marry. It's better to marry than
> to burn with lust.
>
> 1 Corinthians 7:1–2, 9

Scriptures teach that the healthiest sex is between a man and woman who have committed themselves to one another for a lifetime. What is "healthy" sex, anyway? It is what is experienced within the confines of a marriage that goes the distance. It is committed passion that lasts in a marriage for a lifetime. It is a romance that reaches the heights, weathers the storms and survives the fires. Healthy sex is about living out your hopes and dreams, your goals and desires in your relationship with the one you vowed to spend your life with.

This does not mean that if you wait for sex until marriage that all your sexual experiences with your spouse will be perfect. Having healthy married sex does not mean that you will never encounter hard times in your sexual relationship. Healthy sex means you will avoid *unnecessary* suffering. You may still have pain, but you will avoid all the pain that comes from sex outside of marriage.

Sexuality, like anything, takes time to perfect and understand. It is a private world of exploration for you and your spouse. The more public you make your sexuality before marriage with your future spouse (or anyone for that matter), the harder it will be to keep it private and between the two of you after marriage. Sexuality experienced outside of marriage, whether it is with your future spouse or anyone else, hinders future intimacy. These results do not necessarily surface at first. Nonetheless, over a lifetime, the suffering will become obvious to you and your spouse (unless, of course, you do not recognize it due to denial, unawareness or unwillingness to admit the truth).

If you are careful to protect you and your future spouse from arousing sexual love before it is time, then you will know when it is time to get married. If you use your dating days to learn how to verbally and emotionally communicate, then you will learn more about this person than you ever could if your relationship was blurred by sex.

Once you have the foundation of marriage in your relationship, you can build the framework for an amazing sex life. (It may actually surprise you what the Ancient Scriptures say about this, but we will save that for the next chapter!)

Our Story

We will never forget our wedding night. We awoke the morning of April 24th, 1993, as virgins, and we awoke the morning of April 25th as, well, not virgins. That was the greatest night of our lives, not because the sex was all that great, but because we had waited and allowed our yearnings to be shaped by self-control, boundaries, vulnerability and—most of all—love.

Waiting until marriage for our first sexual experience did not make it perfect, but it did make it profound and amazing. We minimized the sexual baggage that we brought into

Kelly and Tosha Williams

our honeymoon suite, either from history together or histories created apart.

Redeeming Your Story

What is your sexual story? Does your sexual history include only your spouse in your marriage? Have you followed the guideposts in your life and relationship? Did you ignore them? Maybe you did not even know these guideposts exist.

Whatever you have done, wherever the consequences have taken you, the Creator wants to redeem the pages of your life and restore you as a person and as a couple. Because of His amazing redemption, you will be able to write new chapters in your story together. These new chapters will have pages of hope and joy and peace in your relationship. God's redemption is part of the greater Story behind your story.

Regardless of how you heeded the guideposts in your past, you can begin to acknowledge them in your relationship in your present. Do not try to navigate the road of marriage without help. *Embrace Spiritual Guideposts* in your marriage, and they will guide you on the path to REAL.

And, by the way, the guideposts get more inviting in the next chapter, as we look at what the Ancient Scriptures say about sex and marriage. Take a deep breath, because this is where "Fantasy Meets Reality."

Discussion Questions:

As with all the other chapters of this book, we encourage you to spend time with your spouse processing the following questions. You may want to think through them individually and then talk about them together.

1. What sexual guideposts did you follow in your dating relationship? Why? What positives do you see in your current relationship because of this?

2. What guideposts did you not follow? Why? How has this affected your relationship?

3. What can you do to redeem your sexual history? What causes you to doubt it can be redeemed? Do you believe the Creator can redeem these pages of your story? If you doubt He can, why?

4. How can these guideposts begin to matter to you now? For example, is there any existing sexual activity such as pornography that you need to remove from your life today? How could this make room for hope, joy and peace in your "story of us"?

5. The Ancient Scriptures say you are made for more than sex. You were made to experience your Creator's presence. If you have never engaged Him in relationship, ask Him to reveal Himself to you today. We know He will. If you are a believer, talk to Him right now about your present, your past, your life and your marriage. He deeply cares about you.

Kelly and Tosha Williams

7. the crossroads

> *"We shall create a thousand strands, great and small,*
> *that will link us together."*
> - from *A Severe Mercy* by Sheldon Vanauken

Our marriage has encountered many crossroads along the way. For us, so far, marriage has been a fourteen-year story. In 1993, we graduated from college; in 1996, we completed seminary. In 1997, we bought our first home and birthed our first child.

In 2001, we sold our first home and bought our second home. In 2005, we sold that house and bought our current home. In 1999, 2002, 2004 and 2007, we added four more children to our family.

These are the crossroads, the big moments of our lives. At the crossroads of where to live, we came to Colorado. At the crossroads of what to accomplish with our lives, we decided to start Vanguard Church. At the crossroads of having children, we chose to have five. These highlights have earned chapter titles in our life's story along the way.

A thousand other words and pages in each chapter have been crossroads for us, as well. Filling each of the big moments are countless smaller ones that have been just as important in the direction of our relationship. The choices we have made and the decisions we continue to make each day at each of these crossroads will affect our marriage until death do us part.

In order to *Embrace Spiritual Guideposts* at the daily crossroads we face in marriage, then we must know what the Ancient Scriptures teach for marriage. After all the "do nots" of the guideposts in the last chapter, these marriage guideposts at the crossroads are where fantasy can begin to meet reality in your relationship.

Marriage Guidepost Number One: Live as One!

"I now pronounce you man and wife." That proclamation at our wedding ceremony was an exhilarating moment, just as it certainly was at yours. We had walked to the wedding altar separately, but, after this proclamation, we walked out of our ceremony arm in arm, together. We had become one, a unit in the eyes of God and society.

The Ancient Scriptures tell us that the Creator made marriage to be this way. Consider these words:

> Husbands ought to love their wives as they love their own bodies. For a man who loves his wife actually shows love for himself. No one hates his own body but feeds

and cares for it... As the Scriptures say, 'A man leaves
his father and mother and is joined to his wife, and the
two are united into one.' This is a great mystery...

Ephesians 5:28, 29, 31

When you become married, the Ancient Scriptures teach
that you become "one flesh." What in the world does this
mean? It is a hard concept to understand, but it is a small
wonder that our minds can hardly grasp the concept. Even
Scripture admits that this is a *great* mystery. Mystery or not,
though, the truth is that your marriage was not made for two
coinciding manuscripts of "the story of *me*." Instead, every
marriage should be its own unique "story of *us*."

This is a choice, though. As you seek to live as one, you
face a crossroads every day of your relationship. At each
crossroads, you must make a choice. You will pick one of the
following two routes.

The Crossroads

You Will Live As One:	You Will Live as Two:
You are your spouse's greatest ally and advocate. You consider your spouse's ideas, thoughts and needs as important as your own. You battle *for* each other.	You are either roommates with separate lives or enemies who continually oppose one another. You must fend for yourself, whether that is emotionally, physically, spiritually or relationally.

Which route will you go at the crossroads? Which direction is your marriage going today? Do you know why?

We face this crossroads every time we are in an argument. Will we each fight for our own rights? Or, will we battle *for* each other? Will Tosha seek what is best for herself, or will she seek what is best for Kelly?

We face this crossroads when there are chores to be done that are normally part of the other person's responsibility. Will Kelly go watch television while Tosha finishes her work alone, or will he pitch in and help her get it done?

We face this crossroads in every aspect of our marriage. Will we live for ourselves and demand our own priorities? Or, will we live as one and figure out what works best for both of us and meets both of our needs?

Some couples choose not to live as one. These are the couples who overly criticize each other in front of other people. These are the marriages in which spouses live as roommates, with intentionally separate schedules, bank accounts or social lives. These are the relationships where both spouses must fend for themselves.

Marriages such as this become neglectful, critical and, often, downright harmful. It is a lonely, painful way to live. You are one, but you function as two.

The other route at the crossroads is to live as one in marriage. In our opinion, this route is much more appealing. Really, it is the reason we got married in the first place. We chose to go to that wedding ceremony because we *wanted* to be together. We *wanted* to encounter life together. We *wanted* to be each other's safe place in this world.

Nevertheless, when we encounter the crossroads, we still

Kelly and Tosha Williams

have to *choose* to live as one. When you choose to live as one, you will care for your spouse like you care for yourself. You will nurture your marriage just as you nurture your own body. Living as one in REAL marriage creates an indivisible unity in which the team is even more important than each individual player.

Having grown up in Kentucky, I am an avid fan of college basketball, especially the Kentucky Wildcats. I watch every Kentucky game televised in Colorado. I proudly wear my "blue" sweatshirts and let everybody know that Kentucky is *my* team. In the same way, when I live as one with Tosha, I am her biggest fan and, at times, her most concerned coach or sports therapist. Nobody cares about the way she plays life as much as I do, because, after all, we are on the same team. In fact, in REAL marriage, we *are* the team.

You and your spouse should be *the team* in your marriage, too. For the sake of your marriage, choose to live as one at the crossroads.

Marriage Guidepost Number Two: Enjoy Sex!

At some point in life, most people like sex because it feels good. The Ancient Scriptures do not deny this; in fact, Scriptures teach that sex can make you come alive and fill you with passion in marriage. The Scriptures paint this sensual scene:

> I am my lover's, and he claims me as his own. Come, my love, let us go out to the fields and spend the night among the wildflowers. Let us get up early and go to

the vineyards to see if the grapevines have budded, if the blossoms have opened, and if the pomegranates have bloomed. There I will give you my love. There the mandrakes give off their fragrance, and the finest fruits are at our door, new delights as well as old, which I have saved for you, my lover.

Song of Songs 7:10–13

We are not trying to be sacrilegious, but, if this passage were a movie, we think it might get an R-rating. Disguised in the flowery language is an unambiguous call for sexuality. Believe it or not, the Ancient Scriptures advocate sex under the stars! Whether it is love on the beach, out in the meadow or back in the garden, this guidepost is a flashing sign for married couples: Go for it! Remember your fantasies! Live them! Enjoy them! Create new ones!

However, you must make a decision at this crossroads, too. Which route will you choose?

The Crossroads

You Enjoy Sex:	You Don't Enjoy Sex:
You engage each other, are hot for each other, tantalize and fulfill each other.	You let your marriage become boring, mundane and ho-hum.

Do you enjoy sex with your spouse? Come on, be honest. *Do you enjoy it?* Do you look forward to it? Couples face this crossroads every day in their physical creativity. We have all seen boring, ho-hum marriages. You do not have to know what goes on (or does not go on) in the bedroom to tell when couples are plain bored with each other.

While marriage cannot normally maintain unceasing sexual rapture, it *can* be filled with a lot of excitement. It all boils down to the choices you make with each other. What do you do in your marriage to keep sex fresh?

Think about the best sex the two of you have experienced in the past—ponder it, remember it, romanticize it—in order to set the stage for the "next time." Wife, do you want to enjoy sex with your husband more? Then anticipate the sex you are going to have—fix your hair, wear a nighty, spray perfume, light candles. If you are married, the Creator designed sex to be enjoyed by you and your spouse. Are you taking advantage of the opportunity?

Years ago on our honeymoon, we read *The Act of Marriage* by Tim and Beverly LaHaye. As we drove the many miles from Virginia to our Seaside destination in Florida, we read the pages aloud. We laughed a lot; we learned a lot. That book was a helpful starting point for us.

On our tenth wedding anniversary, another book came our way. *Sheet Music*, by Dr. Kevin Leman, is all about married sex. We packed this book in our bags as we left our children in the care of friends and family and headed to Mexico for an anniversary trip. Every night on that trip, we enjoyed dinner at a little Mexican restaurant by the beach. We ate, talked and dreamed to the sound of the crashing waves, and then we lingered over dessert long after watching the sunset.

While every evening was romantic and magical, every day of that trip was fun. We would claim our spot by the pool and, between dips in the water and walks on the beach, bask in our lounge chairs to read *Sheet Music*. One of us would read a few pages then pass the book over to the other. We reeled with laughter at times as we processed Dr. Leman's witty observations about sex. In very candid ways, he gave us a refresher course on how to be sexually creative in our marriage.

Are you enjoying sex with your spouse? If not, maybe you need a vacation—away from the kids! Maybe you need to plan an anniversary trip or a just-because trip. Maybe you should just pick up a copy of *Sheet Music* or another book that teaches you how to enjoy sex with your spouse based on the guideposts of Scripture.

This stuff makes for good date-night conversation. Just do not be surprised when other people in the restaurant are looking at you, trying to figure out what is so funny!

Marriage Guidepost Number Three: Keep Having Sex!

The Ancient Scriptures do not want you to stop having sex. This guidepost points the way and says: *keep doing it*! Consider these verses from the book of Proverbs:

> Let your wife be a fountain of blessing for you. Rejoice in the wife of your youth. She is a loving deer, a graceful doe. Let her breasts satisfy you always. May you always be captivated by her love.
>
> Proverbs 5:18–19

This short passage uses the word "always" twice. *Always* be satisfied with your wife's breasts; *always* be captivated by her love. The time frame here is "happily ever after." Scripture tells us how to live that fairytale we have all dreamed about.

As with the other crossroads, you have a choice for which route your marriage will go.

The Crossroads

You Keep Having Sex:	You Don't Keep Having Sex:
You allow sex to be an amazing way to stay connected with your spouse. You create new ways for "Fantasy Meets Reality" to happen in your marriage.	You let life get in the way and miss out on this important connection. You are stuck in the "Fantasy Versus Reality" or "Fantasy Drowned by Reality" stage.

We personally faced this crossroads every time we were expecting a baby. Pregnancy always did a number on our marriage and especially on our sex life. Would the conception of the child be the last time we enjoyed sex for nine-plus months? Or would we choose to make the most of the opportunities that arose amidst morning sickness, evening sickness, roller-coaster emotions and a swollen belly?

We faced this crossroads when each of our children was born. Overwhelming exhaustion can speak death into anybody's sex life, but especially that of new parents. Would we fall into bed like zombies every night without taking time to connect? Or would we seek to keep enjoying sex after the little by-products of our intimacy came screaming into our lives?

Now, granted, there are some couples who, for physical

reasons, cannot have or keep having sex. We imagine there may come a day when we encounter our own physical barriers to having sex. However, even if a couple cannot actually have sex, they can still find ways to enjoy each other. Every married couple must keep finding ways to stay sexually connected in marriage (and, yes, that pun is fully intended!)

Whether or not you will keep having sex with your spouse is a crossroads you will encounter over and over again. Will you watch *SportsCenter*, or will you go snuggle with your wife? Will you finish the dishes before bed, or will you model that fancy negligee for your husband? Will you succumb to the boring routine in your life, or will you go make out in the hot tub? Do you want to stay in the "Fantasy Versus Reality" stage? Or do you long for "Fantasy Meets Reality" in your marriage?

If the latter option is what you really desire, then what route will you choose at this crossroads of your marriage to get you there? What are you going to do *tonight*?

Marriage Guidepost Number Four: Seek Fulfillment Together

When you live as one, you are not meant to be miserable in your marriage. The Scriptures teach us that the marriage relationship is an avenue through which married people are to find happiness. Consider these words of the wisest person who ever lived, King Solomon:

> Live happily with the woman you love through all the meaningless days of life that God has given you under the sun. The wife God gives you is your

reward for all your earthly toil. Whatever you do, do well ...

Ecclesiastes 9:9–10

God is not a cosmic sadist who wants you to have a boring life. He did not create a beautiful world so that you would never find enjoyment. He did not create marriage to tie you down, nail you to the ground and make you unfulfilled for the rest of your life. While your happiness is not His highest priority, He does want you to find happiness and meaning in your life.

So, at this guidepost is another crossroad, another place where you must choose which route to take in your REAL marriage.

The Crossroads

You Seek Fulfillment Together:	You Don't Seek Fulfillment Together:
You find happiness by working together to make your dreams and fantasies come true.	You find your own happiness apart from, maybe in spite of, your spouse.

One of our favorite marriage analogies comes from the book *A Severe Mercy* by Sheldon Vanauken. In it, the author tells about the relationship he and his wife, Davy, experienced many years ago. The two were convinced that they would live the greatest love ever lived. They were determined to experience that in every aspect of their lives.

One afternoon, the two had an argument that propelled them into a long discussion about the secret to lasting love.

Here is an excerpt from the book that beautifully describes what they realized:

> "Look," we said, "what is it that draws two people into closeness and love? Of course there's the mystery of physical attraction, but beyond that it's the things they share. We both love strawberries and ships and collies and poems and all beauty, and all those things bind us together. Those sharings just happened to be; but what we must do now is share *everything*. Everything!
>
> "If one of us likes *anything*, there must be something to like in it—and the other one must find it. Every single thing that either of us likes. That way we shall create a thousand strands, great and small, that will link us together. Then we shall be so close that it would be impossible—unthinkable—for either of us to suppose that we could ever recreate such closeness with anyone else.
>
> "And our trust in each other will not only be based on love and loyalty but on the *fact* of a thousand sharings—a thousand strands twisted into something unbreakable."

We have taken this "thousand strands" concept into our own marriage, not out of compulsion but out of curiosity. How strong a marriage can we build as we seek fulfillment together? How tight a bond can we form as we reach into each other's life and interests? When each of us makes the other's fantasy our own, then we have another strand that connects us. That is how "Fantasy Meets Reality."

Like Sheldon and Davy, our fantasy is to experience an

enduring love. If togetherness, indeed, is the secret to making love last, then we want to share everything. We want to continually seek new things to bond us together. This leads to valuing new experiences (which we discuss in chapter fifteen).

What type of marriage do you want? Do you want a marriage where you are connected only by your past vows, a very few common interests and a handful of kids? Or do you desire a marriage with a "thousand strands" of happiness and connection? We hope you choose to seek fulfillment together at the crossroads.

Marriage Guidepost Number Five: Keep Sex Sacred

We live in a society where very little is sacred. In our culture, marriage is not sacred, and sex certainly is not sacred. Yet, the Ancient Scriptures establish a counter-cultural guidepost with words like these:

> Drink water from your own well—share your love only with your wife. Why spill the water of your springs in the streets, having sex with just anyone? You should reserve it for yourselves.
> Never share it with strangers.
>
> Proverbs 5:15–17

Scripture teaches that what the two of you share is for the two of you alone. Your sexuality is sacred; will you keep it sacred in your marriage? This is your daily choice at the crossroads.

The Crossroads

You Keep Sex Sacred:	You Don't Keep Sex Sacred:
Your intimacy and sexuality is your private fantasy shared only by the two of you in your marriage.	You invite a third party into your marriage and lead your marriage down to death and ruin.

We face this crossroads of keeping our sex sacred every time we rent a movie or go to the theater. Will we choose movies that introduce a third party in a good light? Or if we start watching something that goes past our boundaries, will we turn it off or walk out?

We are not trying to be legalistic at this crossroads because not every R-rated movie is harmful to our marriage and not every PG-rated movie is okay for our marriage. Keeping sex sacred is a moment-by-moment, day-by-day, decision-making process.

You may face this crossroads daily at your computer. Clicking on pornographic sites, looking at naked women or searching for salacious new sites may be a habit for you. Will you keep doing this, or will you keep sex sacred in your marriage?

Other couples face this crossroads when they feel their sexual relationship is growing stale. It is easy to rationalize away the sacredness of their relationship when it does not feel all that special anyway. So they try to inject new life into their sexuality by exchanging partners, bringing another person into their bedroom or allowing each other a "one-time" affair.

For the record, you cannot keep sex sacred when you

Kelly and Tosha Williams

need a third party—be that television, internet, pornography, another person or couple—to turn you on to each other. Even if the two of you mutually consent to the practice, it destroys the sacredness of your marriage.

If you choose to engage a third party, the Ancient Scriptures teach that you will devastate your life. Consider these words in Proverbs:

> For a prostitute will bring you to poverty, but sleeping with another man's wife will cost you your life. Can a man scoop a flame into his lap and not have his clothes catch on fire? Can he walk on hot coals and not blister his feet? So it is with the man who sleeps with another man's wife. He who embraces her will not go unpunished.
>
> Proverbs 6:26–29

The words of this verse are directed at husbands, but the guidepost speaks to wives, too. If you bring a third party into your relationship, either with or without your spouse's approval, you are demolishing the very foundations of not just your marriage but also your very life. You can go ahead and assure yourself that this will not happen to you. Without a doubt, though, you *will* experience devastating consequences when you violate the sacredness of your marriage. Is that worth it?

If, on the other hand, you choose the route of keeping sex sacred, you will seek out new means to enhance your marriage and make it special. You will look for new ways to get each other hot and turn each other on. (We will talk more about this in the last section of the book.) You will love and enjoy sex within the purity and privacy of your relationship.

Before we leave this crossroads, let us add this. Men do not seem to have a problem talking about sex; women sometimes do. A few years ago, Tosha tried to lead a small women's group through a discussion about enhancing their sexual relationships with their husbands. This group had journeyed together for a year, so intimate conversations were nothing new. Yet, this particular topic suddenly made the group very uncomfortable. It was as if to talk about sex, even in a healthy, constructive way, was to violate the sacredness of it.

Everybody has a level of comfort in sharing about sex. We have gone the extra mile in sharing about our marriage in this book, not because it is entirely comfortable for us, but because we want to lead in REAL marriage. Keeping sex sacred does not mean you can never talk about sex, ask questions about it or seek help for it. Keeping sex sacred means that you honor your spouse and engage in all forms of sexuality with that person only.

The Awaiting Crossroads of Your Story

Just like us, every day you and your spouse make choices in your marriage. Some of the choices you make are the big picture, life-changing crossroads sort, like whether to move, change jobs or have another child.

Still, most of the choices you make are the kind we have talked about in this chapter. They are the everyday crossroads of your lives. Will you and your spouse be unified today? Will you and your spouse have sex? Will you keep doing it?

Will you seek new strands of connection with one another? Will you keep your sexual relationship sacred?

You are continually writing new chapters in your "story of us." What will you fill today's pages with: laughter, arguments, kisses, passionate sex, anger, hurt, another person? We hope your story will be about you and your spouse walking the path for marriage set forth by the Scriptures. This is what *Embracing Spiritual Guideposts* is all about.

Nevertheless, even in choosing the right path at the crossroads of life, we can still find ourselves tripped up by the never-ending opportunities that this world has to offer. In the next chapter, we are going to unpack the poor choices that *all* of us sometimes make at the marriage crossroads and learn how to deal with these.

For Discussion:

Consider the choices you and your spouse make at each of the crossroads we've described in this chapter. Plan a date to talk through each of the marriage guideposts. Here are some additional questions to guide you:

1. What does "one flesh" mean to you? In what ways do you feel like you and your spouse are living as "one flesh"? In what ways do you feel like you are going about marriage separately?

2. Is your marriage a safe place for you? If not, why? If it is, how have you chosen to be each other's safe place this past week?

3. Go back through the chapter and look at the crossroads. What do you think about these crossroads? Are there any

you disagree with? Why? Is there a crossroad where you are struggling? Which one(s)? Why?

4. Have you ever chosen to follow one of the guideposts and found your marriage harmed because of that? When? How?

5. What is your sex life like right now? Do you have sex? How often? Are you really enjoying it? Is your spouse? What can you do to enhance it in coming days?

6. What are some of the "thousand strands" that connect the two of you in your marriage?

7. Thoughts lead to feelings, and feelings lead to actions. If the action you want to experience is great sex, then what thoughts would be helpful to get you there?

8. the confessions

"Once you establish anything truly intimate with another person—even talking—it has to affect the person you're supposed to be the most intimate with."
— *Katie in* The Story of Us

During our seventh year of marriage, our family went on a much-needed vacation. Some time had elapsed since we had been able to get away from our lives' craziness. Finally, though, we were able to unhook and take a break. We live in Colorado, so we decided to take a camping trip through Colorado, to the Tetons and on to Yellowstone National Park. The trip had its shining moments as we discovered new-to-us sights and spectacles. It also had its low moments, like when our eighteen-month-old threw up all over us in our tent—in the middle of the night, no less.

The lowest moment, though, came when Kelly realized

something about his heart. As Kelly pondered whether he would lead our relationship in full disclosure or hide the truth in his heart, our relationship stood at a crossroads.

After camping for days, we stopped off at a hotel for one final night. At that time, we had one child, and Tosha was pregnant with our second. Weary from traveling, we decided to watch a movie in our room and randomly chose one from the hotel stash. The movie was *The Horse Whisperer*, starring Robert Redford as someone who could gently help horses heal.

The movie tells the story of an injured girl and horse who need rehabilitation. When the horse is taken to the horse whisperer's ranch, the little girl and her mother often drive to there to be with the animal. Over time, Redford and the girl's mother become attracted to each other. Although she is married, the two of them connect and almost have an affair. In the end, they refrain, not because they don't want to be together, but because they realize it is wrong.

The two of us had very mixed emotions about the movie. When it was over, I looked at Tosha and asked her about what she thought about it. All I can remember is the harshness of her assessment about any married person who has an affair. Internally, I felt condemned by her words because, just before we watched the movie, I had been outside at a picnic table journaling about my own life. As my pen filled the pages, I discovered, for the first time in my marriage, that I was seriously attracted to someone other than my wife. I was on the verge of choosing the wrong route at the crossroads.

Violating the Guideposts

You do not have to watch television or movies very long before you see the ancient guideposts violated. He cheats on her; she has an affair on him. You do not have to live marriage very long, either, before *you* have the opportunity to violate the ancient guideposts.

We walk the ancient path, follow the guideposts and love each other very much. However, no one, including us, follows the ancient path of REAL perfectly. Nothing guarantees that you will not face temptations, maybe indulge in temptations and eventually have to confess to your spouse.

Every marriage partner will face struggles that require confession. These struggles may be internal thoughts or external actions; they may be sexual or non-sexual in nature. Regardless, every person will have struggles to confess, each of us included. We are not suggesting that our commitment to one another is flippant when we tell you this. Our failures and confessions come with great pain. Honesty about these with each other is a part of our personal path to REAL.

Confession is no easy task. It is almost impossible to look into the eyes of your spouse and confess the truth about your heart. It is embarrassing, shameful and downright humiliating. What will happen when you confess the truth of your heart to your spouse? What will happen if you tell your spouse the secrets of your heart? What will happen if you bring up the failures of your past—or present—so that your spouse will really know you?

When we initially went through this manuscript with a small group at Vanguard Church, one person said, "There is something fully amazing and fully terrifying about being fully known." Ironically, we cannot remember who made this statement, but we fully agree with it. Being known *is* both amazing and terrifying. Being known is what confession is all about.

We want to share with you our confessions not because we have to, but because we choose to in order to give you an example of how to go about confession in your marriage. We also want to encourage you to realize that the extent to which you have followed the spiritual guideposts will largely determine how difficult this task is going to be for your marriage. Why? Because the guideposts are signs of the Creator's presence in your relationship. His presence governs your heart and protects you.

Unfortunately, nobody follows the guideposts perfectly, so we all suffer the effects. Our marriage is no exception.

A Heart Affair

As I journaled at the picnic table then watched the movie, I began to see what was happening in my life. A very deep desire for another woman had taken root in my heart, and I wanted to pursue her with everything inside of me.

I had never acted on this desire; the woman knew nothing of my private thoughts. Still, my heart had grown away from Tosha and to a third party. Coming face to face with this realization broke me, upset me and freed me all at the same time.

How did this happen? How did it happen to *me*? What did I do wrong to get here? How did I become attracted to another woman? I thought I had followed the guideposts for a REAL marriage. Why did the guideposts not protect me?

My mind swirled from myself to Tosha. Seeing her disgust at the potential affair in the movie, everything in me wanted to tear the vulnerable pages from my journal and throw them in the nearby creek. In spite of the temptation, I knew I could not do that. I had to tell Tosha.

What would she think? How will she feel? I did not want to hurt her, but I knew it would.

Rationalization set in. Nothing had happened between this woman and me. The attraction was only in my heart. Why did I need to confess this to Tosha? Why did she even need to know? I could not answer these questions when I had written them in my journal earlier. I just knew that, when the movie ended, I had to tell Tosha. If I did not, a wedge would be established between us and begin creating cracks in our marriage. I valued my relationship with Tosha too much to let that happen.

So, I gave her my journal and told her I needed her to read some things that would be very painful to her. In that hotel room, Tosha sat on one bed and I the other. Our only child played at our feet unaware of the major struggles we were facing.

As I sat there and watched Tosha read, she began to cry and cry and cry. There I was, attracted to another woman while my wife was pregnant. What was my problem? Grow up, right?

No amount of guilt, condemnation or moral pressure could change the reality of our relationship at that time. We had to feel it, deal with it and process it together. I waited in silence as she wept. I remember feeling as if I had hurt my wife in a way that I had never hurt her before. I had crushed her spirit and placed in her heart grief that she was not expecting and did not know how to process.

I expected Tosha to be judgmental at me and angry toward

me, but she was not. She was hurt, upset and, more than anything, confused. She wondered aloud, "Why?" I could not tell her the *why*, only the *what*. She wondered aloud if she had done something to drive me away or if she simply was not appealing enough.

The answer to her questions was "no" but, still, Tosha just cried.

And I wept.

On the Path to REAL

Confession hurts! It hurts your spouse, and it hurts you. However, confession is the only way to begin to *Embrace Spiritual Guideposts* you may have missed along the way in your relationship. Confession is one way you live out the vulnerability that we discussed way back in chapter four.

Remember, vulnerability leads to trust, and trust can lead to greater fantasy. Without vulnerability and without confession, your marriage can never go deeper. Fantasy cannot meet reality if it is hindered by secrets and lies. Furthermore, the longer you wait to confess, the farther you wander from the ancient path of REAL. The farther you wander, the more pain you will have to swim back through to get back to the ancient path of REAL.

We all want to be known fully, but sometimes being known fully means telling something about our lives we would rather not share. The sharing, though, is what can help you find freedom and create trust. Since we have a crisis of trust in relationships, the one way to combat this in marriage is to create a culture of confession.

What is confession? Confession is sharing something about your life with another person. Specifically in this book, confession is telling your spouse about things in your life that he or she does not know. This is never easy. This very well may be one of the hardest things you ever have to do.

However, we want to encourage you that this may be a part of *Realizing the Cost* in your marriage. This may be the very thing you need to do to *Embrace Spiritual Guideposts*. Confession may be the place you need to start in order for your relationship to get back on the ancient path to REAL.

As a couple, we had to circle back to the ancient guideposts for marriage and deal with this struggle in our marriage. We both *Realized the Cost*, for Kelly had to get parts of his heart under control, and Tosha had to forgive. This was a huge growing time for our marriage as we recommitted to *Embrace Spiritual Guideposts* and walk even closer as a couple in the future.

More Confessions

The day came, though, when Tosha's heart proved to be as dangerous as Kelly's was. As upsetting as his struggles had been to me, I soon encountered struggles of my own that I needed to confess. I became attracted to another man who was, in my imagination, everything Kelly was not. I thought about this man, and I got nervous flutters around this person.

Ever so quickly, a stronghold established in my heart to be closer to this man than to Kelly. I was not looking for this struggle; I was not asking for it. Yet, there it was, in all its secret beauty and ugliness because, although I knew it was wrong, I found pleasure in the idea. Nothing on the outside happened, but nothing stopped my inward progression, either.

One night, when Kelly was out of town, I dreamed about this other man. I awakened guilty and mortified at myself. My husband—the man I had committed my life to—was away. Yet, instead of missing him, I was spending time with someone else in my dreams. What a violation of our vows!

I was horrified at my depravity, but I was also fortunate. Because of what we had already experienced in confession in our marriage, I had a template to handle my new struggles. Once I saw where my mind and heart were going, I began to journal.

I have journaled since middle school, and Kelly acquired the habit in college. Today, this is standard practice for both of us, especially when we are struggling with something. Journaling is helpful because many times the pen can confess what your mouth cannot. Going through the exercise of writing down what I was thinking about helped prepare me to better articulate it to Kelly when it was time to tell him.

We had already determined that we were going to share everything in our marriage, even the bad stuff. This is called "full disclosure." Many people balk at this idea; many others ridicule it. In spite of this, we believe that full disclosure is *essential* for REAL marriage. *For your fantasy and reality to meet fully, you cannot have secrets that keep you apart in any way.*

This does not mean that you must confess every graphic detail about your present or past. Full disclosure in marriage means that you must be *willing* to confess every detail that your spouse wants to or needs to know.

From the beginning of our marriage, we established the

Kelly and Tosha Williams

full disclosure rule for our relationship: no secrets. We gave each other the right to know about what is going on in the other's life. In this current situation, "no secrets" meant that I had to tell Kelly about my wayward heart when he got home.

Whatever the nature of confession, the longer you wait, the more pain you create for yourself, your spouse and maybe even your children. In addition, the longer you wait to confess, the more of a stronghold the secret can create in your heart.

I knew I would hurt Kelly by telling him my heart's illicit secret. I realistically expected that he would be upset and bothered. He had every right to feel betrayed. Yet, there is nothing like *both* of you admitting you struggle to put you on equal ground. I could no longer act all high and mighty about the deficiencies in his life ... they were in mine, too.

As soon as we had some private time, I self-consciously told Kelly what was happening in my heart. It was so awkward and embarrassing to have to tell him this, especially after I had made him feel condemned several years prior. Nonetheless, I swallowed my pride and humbled myself to ask his forgiveness. He lovingly forgave me, and we set down the path of making our marriage more "other-proof."

Honesty with Kelly partially released me from the stronghold in my heart. When, as the days and weeks went by, I realized I needed more help, I found accountability. I turned to a trusted friend who could keep my secret and pray for me. I was painfully honest with her. Having somebody besides Kelly *know* the truth helped further release me.

Where We Go From Here

In our experience and observation, there is always something to confess in marriage.

Whether it is a heart affair, a real-life affair, an emotional struggle or an entirely different category of failure, we all mess up. If you want to experience REAL marriage, you must make things right again with your spouse.

Because of this, we have learned in our relationship to consistently share our struggles with each other rather than let them build up. What should you confess to your spouse? In our marriage, we live by the "parameter of three." I confess anything to Tosha that I cannot stop thinking about after three days. I assume if I cannot stop thinking about someone or something in that amount of time, that means it may be on its way to becoming a problem.

Tosha lives by the "parameter of three," as well. Instead of going by three days, however, she goes by three times: three illicit dreams, three series of unbidden thoughts, three wrong glances, et cetera. This is how she keeps a check in her life.

In our marriage, we confess our thoughts and dreams to one another, and we allow each other to read our journals at any time. These are all ways that we "other-proof" our marriage. We are committed to doing whatever it takes to keep the reality of our relationship safe so that our fantasy can grow strong.

This culture of confession has been created over a period of time in our marriage. Do not automatically expect that your wife will be willing to let you read her journal or that your husband is going to tell you all his dreams. Instead of immediately imposing parameters on one another, give your marriage freedom to grow in this area. You can slowly begin

Kelly and Tosha Williams

the process of consistently sharing by starting a regular time, maybe weekly or bi-weekly, where you sit down and talk about your struggles.

You may not know *what* to share with your spouse. Some questions are at the end of this chapter that you can use to help create an environment of trust in your marriage. If you are still in doubt about what to tell, remember that wisdom can come through a multitude of counselors, so seek advice before you share if necessary.

The bottom line is: *we believe that it is much better for your marriage for you to tell your struggles than to act them out.* Instead of having to say to your spouse someday, "I had an affair," confess to your spouse now, "I am attracted to this person, and I need your help to get over it." Let your spouse then dictate to you how you will or will not be in relationship with that person. Allow your spouse to establish guidelines around you in your struggle. Though this may sound like control, it actually serves to protect your marriage and rebuild trust.

Trust takes time, just as full disclosure marriage and culture of confession do. You cannot go without it for years then all the sudden decide you will have it. Trust is organic and grows with time. Give it a chance to grow by honestly and vulnerably sharing with your spouse.

Just as trust takes time, healing does, too. It is a bad idea to try to resolve instantly the issues brought up in a culture of confession. Talk about the issues, wrestle with them and get help for them if necessary. But, most importantly, give your spouse and your marriage time to deal with the pain.

Danger Zones

As you share the raw data of your life with your spouse, it is important to do something pro-active with that information. Every marriage has danger zones, so that is where you must begin building protective boundaries for your relationship. Do not wait until you have fallen off a precipice in your life before you build a wall that will keep you away from the edge. You must figure out what boundaries are necessary to keep your marriage safe. Establish those boundaries and always respect them.

Another proactive way to protect your relationship is to have accountability outside your marriage. Identify a person, other than your spouse, with whom you can have *total* disclosure regarding your struggles. This person may be your leader or someone who is accountable with you. Share your ongoing struggles with this person instead of continually dumping those issues on your spouse. This can help minimize the negativity in your marriage.

We are not saying that because you have an accountability partner you should not share things with your spouse. We are simply saying that it is often unhealthy to make your spouse your *primary* or *only* accountability partner. Confess to your accountability partner your struggles. However, if you cross a boundary and have secrets you are keeping, you must then go ahead and confess those things to your spouse. Give your accountability partner the authority to press you to confession when you have crossed a line.

It may be that you need more than an accountability partner, boundaries and a culture of sharing to help you with your struggles. If you find yourself not being able to work through your struggles, temptations or issues, you ought to seek more advanced help. A professional counselor or a pastor may be able to help you discuss and deal with the issues that you are facing. Do not be afraid—or too prideful—to ask for help. If you do not find help the first place you ask, look elsewhere and ask again. Your marriage is worth it.

Confession to the Creator

Your marriage may initially go through extremely hard times as you go through the exercise of confession. Your relationship may take some hard hits for a while as you begin to create a culture of sharing. *"Other-proofing" your marriage is not necessarily easy at first.*

Still, we want to encourage you not to give up. A relationship—any relationship, really—that has gone through the fire and survived is a refined relationship, one that can be deeper, more meaningful and more valuable because of the flames. We usually throw away garbage, but we try to restore what is valuable. Be encouraged to see your marriage as a treasure.

As you see your marriage this way, we encourage you to re-engage sexually if you have stopped. Your marriage cannot forever take physical disconnection from one another. No matter how badly the confessions have hurt, do not forever quit having sex. Do not withhold sex as a way to punish your spouse. Start re-engaging each other on a physical level.

Finally, if you have violated the guideposts, be honest with the Creator about what happened. (He already knows, by the way.) Do not pretend that something did not happen or that what you felt is not real. Confess to your Creator a prayer something like this:

> "God, please forgive me for violating the ancient guideposts. I want to experience REAL marriage with my spouse. Help me deal with this issue in my life so that it will not be a stronghold in the future. Give us the ability to deal with the pain I have caused our marriage. Your guideposts teach that You care about this part of my life. So, I ask You to help me make things right again. Amen."

Confession to your Creator and to your spouse is a part of the path to REAL. We admit, being known in this way can be "fully terrifying," as the earlier quote stated. Yet, full disclosure within the realm of marriage can also be "fully amazing," as you reap the benefits of vulnerability and create new layers of trust within your relationship.

We encourage you to take the risk and "go there" in your marriage.

Finally...

Our goal is to keep a short account with each other about our thought lives because this is where affairs begin. When we confess our illicit thoughts to one another, it is less likely that we will ever end up having to confess illicit actions. When we confess, though, it often creates tension in our marriage that turns into conflict. In REAL marriage, how do we work through these difficult times?

In the next section, we will talk about this very thing. The

Kelly and Tosha Williams

next step on the journey to REAL is to *Align Your Will*. In section three, we will unpack the ways we fight as individuals and discover new ways to battle as couples. For fantasy and reality to meet, we must walk together down the ancient path of REAL.

For Discussion:

The following questions are a starting point for creating a culture of confession in your marriage. These questions may initially create conflict. They can also lead to an environment of trust that will enable your marriage to breathe during the hard times.

It is important that you go the extra mile and actually ask your spouse these questions. It is a cop out to rationalize that if your partner wanted to know then he would ask. Be proactive in creating a sharing environment, for the sake of your spouse and your marriage.

You may need to start slowly with these questions, perhaps by discussing a few each time you share in the next month. Talk openly about struggles consistent to the trust you have been able to build in your relationship. For example, if you have been married for a long time and have an environment of trust, you can probably go through these questions more quickly. If you have only been married a short time, or if you have never had a culture of confession, you need to allow your relationship time to incorporate the weight of these questions.

Be encouraged! Although trust is not built in a day, it can be built. So take some time to sit down and start talking— and listening.

1. What does "full disclosure" mean to you? To your spouse?

2. On a scale of zero to ten, what is the culture of confession in your marriage? If zero is "total secrets" and ten is "full disclosure," where are you? Why? How can you create a better culture of confession in your marriage?

3. How have you dealt with secrets in the past? How can you do a better job confessing secrets in the future?

4. Have you established parameters for confession in your marriage? How do each of you keep a check on your life?

5. Are you struggling with something that you need to tell your spouse about? If there is, maybe start with words like these: "I need your help to get over and break free from an issue. Will you help me in this struggle?"

6. Is there anything you have done to give your spouse reason to distrust you? Have you pushed your spouse away? What should you do about this?

7. Talk about whether either of you value someone or something more than each other in your marriage. Then discuss what you can do to make your marriage "other-proof."

8. Do you feel close to each other emotionally? Physically? Sexually? What can you do to make your marriage feel more connected?

9. Have you violated any of the boundaries you have created for each other? If so, how? (Ask yourself, why?) Are there any new boundaries you should create for one another so that your trust can have a chance to grow?

10. Right now, give your spouse the opportunity to tell you or ask

you anything. If this causes a fight, take it easy on each other. We will deal with how to handle conflict in the next section.

Section Three:

Align Your Will

9. the battles

"Marriage is about two people becoming one;
the question is, 'Which one?'"

- Unknown

There are times when you feel the heat in your relationship—and not the good kind. The sparks may begin to fly when you are coming home from the in-laws,' when you head exhausted to bed or when you cannot figure out a compromise on the budget. The fire may erupt when you are trying to have a long-needed conversation or attempting to make love. Suddenly, one little spark ignites an explosion that leaves you both burned and bloody on the battleground.

This happened the day we began writing this chapter. There we were, sitting in a coffee shop, computer plugged in and ready to go. Time was of the essence; we had a brief window to get a lot accomplished. Then a fireball exploded and a battle began.

Truth be told, this battle was because of an unfinished battle from our past. In the month prior, Kelly had been gone a lot. His travels took him all over the globe while I was left behind caring for our young children without a break. When Kelly came home, I made sure he could feel the heat as he prepared to leave on another trip.

In the midst of this was a highlight I wistfully antici-pated: Mother's Day. In my imaginings, it was going to be the perfect day when we were going to all be together as a family and I was going to feel beautiful, beloved and con-nected to my husband and family.

Mother's Day started out great, with Kelly helping the kids serve me breakfast in bed and clean the house. Unfortunately, from my perspective, the day went downhill from the moment my toes touched the floor. I will spare you the details, which include, amongst other things, a runaway dog, missing chocolate-covered strawberries and ugly shoes. By the end of the day, I was fit to be tied and Kelly was the object of my wrath. I hurt him, and he hurt me. The flames of conflict just kept getting hotter.

The day ended, as all bad days eventually do. Soon thereafter, when I left Tosha and the kids again for another business trip, I had plenty of time between meetings to decompress. In that alone time, I was able to process what had happened and move on to the next thing. Tosha, on the other hand, was (with good reason) still caught up in the past while she was consumed with the present. She did not have time to process our battle while I was gone because she was overwhelmed with caring for the home front.

So there we were, finally back together, sitting in a coffee shop and set up to work on this book. I was ready to move on, write a chapter and get something accomplished. Tosha was ready to debrief, talk through it and *then* work on this chapter. I was exhausted from travel; Tosha was exhausted from caring for our family. I wanted to accomplish; she wanted to talk. So, like an explosion, our wills collided. Like on Mother's Day, neither of us cared to align our will to the other.

When Tosha brought up the subject of the past weekend, her words came out more like an attack than an expression of her wounds. On the other hand, I was tired and completely uninterested in rehashing the past. I wanted Tosha to get over it.

We were supposed to work on this book, but all we could do was argue. Over bagels and coffee, the flames were licking at our emotions. Before we started making a scene in the coffee shop, we headed to the truck so we could verbally duke it out in private.

Some couples may give each other the silent treatment when they are mad. Our philosophy is: if it is worth saying, it's worth saying *louder*. So, in the relative privacy of the truck, we argued *loudly*. Tosha's strategy was to tell me how much I had hurt her then run for cover before I could attack her back. My goal was to win, and I would know I had won when I had determined who was right and shut Tosha up.

We both reached our goals: we both won. Yet, in "winning," we left each other burned and bloody on our battlefield. Each of us hurt the person we love the most. Instead of putting out the sparks and diffusing the fires, we had fanned the flames with our words and our anger.

We had not rescued one another from the fire; we had pushed each other into it.

The Battlegrounds

If marriage is all about two people becoming one, then there are two people in every marriage with a very big challenge. Some days the challenge is greater than other days. This idea of becoming one has everything to do with the third part of REAL: *Align Your Will.* When you are angry at each other, when sparks are flying and when the flames of conflict are scorching your relationship, how do you "become one" then?

In the pages that follow, we want to see what creates the sparks of conflict in your marriage. We want to analyze the internal emotions that lay behind your external conflict. If you can learn how to put out the fires before they ignite on your battlegrounds, then you can minimize the damage to your relationship.

First of all, we want to help you figure out where your battlegrounds are. What are the conflicts you most commonly face in your relationship? While a disappointing Mother's Day may be no big deal to you, there *are* things that make you ready to shoot your spouse. What are the issues that send you and your spouse into battle? What are the issues that make you look at your spouse and silently ponder, who *are* you?

In the movie *Shrek,* he and Princess Fiona battle over whether they are going to be beautiful people or green people.

Kelly and Tosha Williams

The movie *Unfaithful* dramatically illustrates the story of a husband and wife who are drifting away from one another sexually—with devastating consequences. In *The Story of Us*, Ben and Katie battle over each other's quirks, nuances and personality traits that are driving them to the point of divorce.

What are the battlegrounds of your marriage? In what areas do you experience the most conflict? There are many possibilities, including:

- Family relationships–blended families; in-laws
- Finances–not enough money; creating a budget; following a budget
- Employment–not enough time away from work; bringing work home; stress from responsibilities; needing a job
- Sexuality–submitting to your spouse's needs; violations of the guideposts
- Communication–appropriately expressing feelings, desires, needs and disappointments
- Expectations–too high or too low
- Relational Issues–old friends; finding friends; needing friends as a couple
- Schedule–little down time; time management; use or misuse of free time
- Conflict resolution–not taking responsibility; unwillingness to forgive; never asking forgiveness
- Children–different parenting approaches; discipline

Of course, this list is not all-inclusive but merely a starting point to get you thinking about what consistently draws you into battle. You may find that your biggest battles are not on

this list but are, rather, one of those icebergs that you identified back in chapter two of this book.

Over the years, you may consistently fight about the same
things or your battlegrounds may change a bit. Family relationships were our biggest challenge at the beginning of our
marriage; finances were our major conflict five to ten years into
marriage. Now, fourteen years into marriage, we tend to fight
most because of the overwhelming schedules in our lives.

Please note, we are not asking you, at this point, what
you *argue* about. Some couples say they never argue, and that
may be the case. You may not argue, but you *do* have conflict.
Whether out loud for all to hear or hushed in the angered
parts of our souls, we all have conflict, so we all must be in the
process of *Aligning Your Will* to one another in that conflict.
The alternative is to head down paths of resentment which
lead ultimately to destruction and possibly even divorce.

The Sparks of Battle

So, you know what your battlegrounds are; you are certainly
aware of what you and your spouse regularly fight about. But
do you know *why* you have these conflicts?

Now, it *is* possible to walk into the battlegrounds of your
marriage and *not* experience conflict. If you can walk into
those realms of your life without unloading the ammunition,
you may not ignite any fires. For example, family relationships may be a continual battle for your marriage. Then, one
Christmas you may be able to spend an entire week visiting
the in-laws without any fires igniting in your marriage. If

this happens, we would guess it is because you did not get the dynamite out of your suitcase.

In our marriage, we can sometimes endure a particularly crazy schedule without sparking a conflict. Though we are in a battleground of our marriage, we do not experience the heat of conflict when we do not unpack the sparks.

Unfortunately, the things that spark battles in our marriage usually hop out of our baggage whether we want them to or not. There are times when everywhere we go, we are a battle waiting to happen. We imagine this might be true of you, too.

See, in the battle you have the external issue—the battleground—that you fight about, and you also have the internal issue—the spark—that motivates the fight. The battleground is the "what" and the spark is the "why" of your conflict; this is true of *every* battle. Every battle has an external and internal impetus. There are the external things, like kids or finances or sex, which you fight about. Then there are the deeper, internal causes that light the fires of those fights.

Do you ever feel like you and your spouse fight all the time (whether verbally or through the silent treatment or some way in between) but never get anything resolved? It may be because you are battling the external stuff when the internal is where the war really rages. While you war about the surface, external things, the true battleground burns in your heart. *The internal sparks are the "why" of conflict.* Until you know why you are fighting, you will never make any progress in the battle.

In our marriage, we have certain things that spark conflict in our battlegrounds. These are often the precursors to conflict for us. Some of our sparks are:

- Unforgiveness
- Fatigue
- Displaced emotions
- Selfishness
- Insensitivity
- Unawareness
- Neglect
- Busyness

If we are near one of our battlegrounds and if one or more of these sparks are with us, then we can easily detonate into an all-out war and find ourselves in the heat of a conflict.

For instance, as we mentioned earlier, our unforgiving schedule is a battleground for us at this point in our marriage. Often there is nothing that can be done about this except to survive the week or get through the month. The problem is that usually a few of the sparks get thrown into this battleground. Displaced emotions about other issues may start the fire, and the angst of insensitivity begins to fan the flames. When a dose of fatigue is poured over the battleground like gasoline, then—boom!—we have a full-blown conflict on our hands.

Understanding Your Sparks

So what about you? What gets you going? You know where your battlegrounds are; you recognize what the sparks are. Once you have identified these things that create conflict in your marriage, though, what are you supposed to do? We encourage you to learn how to *Align Your Will* to one another. One way you can do this is by honestly addressing some pertinent questions which will help you better understand your motivations behind conflict.

The important thing for you and your spouse is to unpack these questions and discuss them *outside* of conflict. Few marriages, ours included, are strong enough to be able to stop in the midst of a heated battle and logically ask productive questions.

However, if you are at least familiar with the concept that behind the external fight may be an internal struggle, then your marriage may be able to gain the upper hand on the conflict before it knocks you down for the count. Mentally moving from *what* you are battling to *why* you are battling can make a huge difference.

We are not saying, by the way, that addressing the internal conflict (or "sparks") will make the external conflict go away. It may or may not; it won't if it really is an external conflict. If your conflict *is* internal, though, you will be able to move the other issues out of the way and deal with what really matters.

So, here are some questions to ask.

"Is there something I cannot forgive you for?"

This is a number one spark in the battleground for many couples. Unforgiveness is a spark that causes enormous fires. Because they have hurt feelings and cannot forgive, they carry the spark with them wherever they go. Then, when they enter a battleground—be it finances or sexuality or expectations—they hardly step a foot in before an explosion occurs.

Is there something for which you cannot forgive your

spouse? If so, ask yourself, *why?* This will define the real battle. Maybe you are afraid that your husband is going to hurt you again. Maybe you do not think your wife is truly sorry for what she did to you. Perhaps your spouse made you experience your greatest fear and you do not think you will ever be able to let that go. Maybe you cannot forgive simply because you are too prideful.

Think about why you cannot forgive your partner. Then, if you are willing to be vulnerable with your spouse, we suggest that you verbalize these feelings and perceptions to your spouse. This might help you further identify the fear that keeps you from being able to forgive your spouse and begin trusting again.

Knowing what your hurt feelings are and recognizing why you cannot forgive, will give you opportunity to diffuse sparks within your marriage. This will help you deal with the real internal battle instead of the external one you may be arguing about.

"Are either of us fatigued right now?"

At this time in our marriage, fatigue is probably the biggest reason why we have conflict. Our schedules and our responsibilities are so demanding that we seldom get to slow down and take a break. There are days and weeks when we feel like we are robots.

You may know exactly how we feel. If you do, then you know that it is easy to have a pity party when you are fatigued. This can lead to words and accusations about things that sometimes do not even matter that much. You express them anyway because, at the time, it seems to help you deal with the fatigue. Whether your fatigue is emotional, relational or physical, exhaustion dulls your mind and sharpens your tongue. These can be devastating when you are in battle.

Knowing how quickly this ignites the fires of conflict for us, we have learned to limit our words to one another when we are tired. We do this because, more often than not, our words are going to be critical or negative toward one another.

When we recognize the spark of fatigue, saying "I am so tired" is an admission of reality rather than defeat. We might follow those words with "I love you and I care about you, but let's talk in the morning." Instead of staying up for hours fighting about stuff that would not even matter if we were both rested and refreshed, we affirm each other and go to bed. When the sun shines again, we may pick up where we left off. Or rest may have extinquished the spark so that we do not even need to talk about it.

"Is one of us displacing emotion right now?"

Sometimes, having a hard day with my personal issues is enough of a spark for me to get mad at Kelly when he gets home. I am not initially annoyed at Kelly, but I *am* upset. Since I may not be able to do anything about that anger in its original context, I do the next best thing. I take it out on the person I feel safest with: Kelly! When I bring that emotion into our marriage—ta-da!—a battle begins.

This is an example of displaced emotion. In marriage, this is when you have conflict with someone or something else, are not able to resolve the issue and then bring the emotion of it into your marital relationship.

Recognizing displaced emotion is a huge step toward diffusing it. When you feel it in your heart, it is essential to *express* it to your spouse rather than take it out on your spouse. If it is appropriate, talk about what has happened and why you are in a bad mood, but do not make this your spouse's fault. If you cannot talk to your spouse without blaming it on him or making it her fault, then make some space between the two of you to create a buffer zone until the negative emotions subside. Letting conflict outside your marriage become conflict inside your marriage is self-defeating.

When you recognize your spouse beginning to displace emotion on you, you have a choice to make. Either you can react in anger which will enable the negative emotion to spark a battle between the two of you. Or you can diffuse the spark by making it distinct from your marriage. Give your spouse the opportunity to be frustrated at life without receiving it as a personal attack on you.

"Am I being selfish?"

Identifying your selfishness is where the rubber meets the road in marriage. In our relationship, when we are both fatigued and frustrated (which is the case more often than we care to admit), each of us tends to become more selfish. It truly becomes survival of the fittest, and selfishness begins popping up everywhere. Maybe you can identify with us if you have ever used phrases like: "*I* want some alone time, so *you* do the dishes and put the kids to bed tonight" or "*I* can't take it anymore so I'm leaving" or "*I'm* mad so you can just deal with it."

Selfishness arises for all kinds of reasons besides fatigue and frustration. If you are being selfish, you can greatly help your marriage by stopping and asking why you are acting that way. To diffuse this spark, you may find it helpful to review the dance steps from chapter four. The music of fantasy can play in the midst of your reality if both of you are willing and determined to do the dance of being selfless.

"Are either of us neglecting the other?"

Nobody says that, in marriage, you have to be clones of each other. However similar you may be, you and your spouse probably do not have the exact same areas of interest. More than likely, your personal likes and dislikes differ. This is reality; it is normal because you are two different people.

Nevertheless, if there is something intrinsically important to your spouse, for whatever reason, but it is not at all important to you, then you have set the stage for your spouse to feel neglected.

If your spouse communicates that something really matters and asks you to be involved in it on some level, then you have a responsibility to engage. This is one of the "thousand strands" you can create for your relationship. You may not enjoy doing whatever it is, but you do it anyway to make your spouse feel valued.

If you absolutely refuse to engage when your spouse specifically asks you to, then you are neglecting your spouse. We realize this is a very strong statement, but we have seen the truth of this over and over again in marriages we have counseled. Neglect due to disengagement will spark all kinds of conflict in marriage.

Do you feel like there is an area in your life or marriage that your spouse does not care about? On the other hand, is there an area that your spouse says *you* do not seem to care about? If there is, why? Is there a reason why you cannot care about this area of your partner's life? Is it due to fear, resentment, confusion, unawareness or naiveté?

One day, after a particularly sad marriage counseling appointment, Kelly came home and asked me, "Is there an area in your life that you feel like I don't care about?" I appreciated the opportunity to express my needs. By listening to me, Kelly made me feel like I really matter. When he responded proactively to my feelings, we enhanced our understanding of each other and diffused our sparks.

"Am I unknowingly hurting you?"

Sometimes we hurt one another in marriage without even realizing it. There are times in every relationship when a wife is unaware of how she affects her husband and when a husband does not realize how he is hurting his wife. Our souls are fragile. When sickness, pain or difficult life situations hammer us, we often act in ways that we never would when life is not so tough. We become insensitive to those around us because we are personally trying to survive what reality sends our way.

We have experienced this in our marriage. It took us five pregnancies to learn how we affect each other during the

Kelly and Tosha Williams

275+ days of gestation. In our first few pregnancies, we had an awful time in our marriage, primarily because of all the wounding we did without even realizing it. Since I am past child birthing and have the perspective of hindsight, I can now see that I was sometimes mean to Kelly, often because I simply did not feel good or had raging hormones. Because he did not know any better as a new father, Kelly would respond back to me in ways that were not particularly encouraging or helpful. Between the two of us, pregnancy became a regular battleground because of how we unknowingly wounded each other emotionally.

After about three pregnancies, I finally realized that Tosha needed me to give her the benefit of the doubt. Her body was temporarily changing her emotions, and her emotions were impacting me without her even knowing it. Giving Tosha space saved us from many battles as we brought our last two children into the world.

You may need to give your spouse the benefit of the doubt, too. Before you decide that your wife is deliberately trying to hurt you, assume that she is unaware of the pain she is causing. Before you deem your husband a jerk, consider the possibility that he may not even realize what he is doing to you.

After you give the benefit of the doubt, you may need to talk your spouse about being insensitive. You cannot—indeed, you must not—forever internalize all the pain your spouse is causing you without speaking up. You have to communicate, with love and respect, how your partner impacts you.

This harkens back to the concepts of vulnerability in chapter four. It is easier to be angry than to be vulnerable when you have been wronged. It is easier to be defensive than to be vulnerable when you *are* wrong. However, vulnerability from both these directions is a dance that intertwines your reality together with your fantasy. The heartbeat of vulnerability is to be honest about your selfishness as well as about your hurt. Doing this makes your marriage a safe place for the two of you. As we mentioned earlier in this book, when your marriage is a safe and vulnerable place, you will have the perfect environment for "Fantasy Meets Reality."

"Are we too busy?"

Today's lifestyles are notoriously busy. Ask a couple about their schedule, and, odds are, you will hear about a very demanding routine. Ask them about when their last date night was, and you will probably hear silence as they try to remember.

If you are seeing an increase in your battles or conflicts, you should re-evaluate your schedule. Before you try to tackle huge issues in the relationship, plan some time together. You may discover that your conflict is not so much about a specific issue as it is about the fact that you are disconnected.

When your schedules get too busy, it is literally time to create space so you can reconnect. Maybe you can do this merely by sitting at the dinner table and talking about the day's events. Perhaps you should plan a weekend getaway in order to experience quality time. We are personally re-instigating a sacred weekly date night for our marriage. It is amazing how quickly you can lose your connection to each other because of work, kids, stress and a million other things. We do not want disconnection from each other to be our reality, so we are doing everything we possibly can to create strands to draw us back together.

Busyness can create all sorts of sparks in a marriage—and not the good kind. Slowing down and reconnecting can create the sparks of fantasy that every marriage needs to thrive.

If after you have had time reconnecting you still have continual conflict, then obviously busyness is not the reason for the conflict. If this is the case, then you must ask yourselves what other sparks are igniting the battles in your marriage.

Diffusing the Sparks

Any of these sparks, in and of themselves, may not cause an explosion in your battlegrounds. But because life continually takes you into the areas where you struggle, the sparks often *do* create fires. You simply cannot always avoid having problems with your children, paying your bills when the bank account is low or dealing with issues at work. These are the realities of life. Because life continually takes you to your battlegrounds, the opportunities for sparks are constant.

When we had the parking lot battle which we described at the beginning of the chapter, there were multiple sparks involved. We were both fatigued; we were displacing our negative emotions on each other; we had been much too busy. And we were, honestly, both being selfish. The multiple sparks created just the right fodder for our huge explosion, which took so much time and effort to work through. Our battle truly was not about Mother's Day, the business trips or the challenges of family. Miscommunication followed by miscommunication led to our relational rift that felt devastating until we resolved it.

Whatever battles you are facing right now, we believe that being able to recognize the sparks in your lives will help diffuse the explosions. Identifying what your battlegrounds are, as well as understanding what motivates your battles, enables you to more readily deal with your conflict. This is how you begin to *Align Your Will.*

Before going to the next chapter, put down this book, grab a pen and paper or your computer and go to a private spot with your spouse. You may find solitude in your bedroom, in a deserted park or, like us, in an empty parking lot. Wherever you go, make sure it is a place where you can be vulnerable with your spouse. A crowded restaurant or the kitchen table may not be the appropriate place.

Once there, reflect upon the reality of the sparks you are facing right now. Are you both exhausted from your schedule? Are you overwhelmed at work or in a conflict outside your marriage? What are the circumstances surrounding your lives right now that are affecting your marriage? Identify these together; talk about them. Write them down so you can know what your propensities are.

Next, discuss what really makes the two of you battle. If you do not know where to begin or how to express your feelings, think back to your last big argument. It may have happened last month or this morning. You may have long forgotten the issue, or you may have it fresh in your mind. For a time, re-enter that arena. How were you hurt? How did you hurt your spouse?

As hard as it may be, answer these questions aloud, and

give each other the liberty to speak without interrupting. Write or type what your spouse says. It will probably be painful. You will not like to hear it. But then, the pain is as much a part of your story as the joy.

Writing down the circumstances and sparks of your lives, as well as what you are currently battling, is very much a part of your own "story of us." By writing down our conflict (which became the first part of this chapter) and then grappling with the sparks behind it, we were able to deal with a painful part of our lives. Seeing, in writing, our battle and the motivations behind our battle has helped us become more proactive in *how* we battle.

Instead of engaging each other head-on like mortal enemies over our external battles, we are learning to fight the sparks together. Instead of fighting *against* each other, we can battle *for* each other. As we will see in chapters to come, this is a part of REAL marriage that creates the opportunity for "Fantasy Meets Reality."

For Discussion:

1. How do you know when you have "won" a fight?

2. Going back to the list of battlegrounds listed earlier in this chapter, which areas are your biggest conflicts in marriage?

3. Of the sparks we described, which ones do you see lighting the fires of conflict in your marriage?

4. *The spark of unforgiveness*: What can you not forgive your spouse for?

5. *The spark of fatigue*: Are one of you or both of you exhausted right now?

6. *The spark of displaced emotion*: Are either of you displacing your emotions right now? How? Why?

7. *The spark of selfishness*: Are you being selfish in your marriage? How?

8. *The spark of neglect*: Is there an area in your life that you do not feel like your spouse cares about? What is it? What areas does your spouse want you to care more about? How can you better show your spouse that you care?

9. *The spark of insensitivity*: Ask your spouse how you may be unknowingly hurting him or her. Be willing to listen to the answer instead of defend yourself.

10. *The spark of busyness*: Are you and your spouse too busy to stay connected? What should you do about this? How can you adjust your lifestyle?

Kelly and Tosha Williams

10. the defensive

"Ben and I are, uh, separated...
(I'm so sorry. How long?)
Um, 72 hours, 4 weeks, 5 years, depending when you
start counting."
- Katie and friend in The Story of Us

Have you ever had a huge fight with your spouse right before company came over for dinner? You were seething with anger toward one another, but you had to swallow your angst and put on a smile—for a whole evening. Ever experienced this? We did just last night. It was awful having to act as if everything was fine.

There is a world of married couples who live this way every day. By appearances, you may never know it because they show up to parties together, they attend church and school programs together and their smiling faces appear side-by-side on family Christmas card pictures.

Yet in their desires, emotions and souls, they live as very different people, separate to the core. While they may still sleep in the same bed, they are facing opposite directions. They may share the same checking and savings account, but their ideas of how to spend their money are diametrically opposed. They may laugh and cheer for the same kid at a little league game, but they have lost their ability to smile at each other.

They are in a battle of the wills. In the midst of a crowded world, these couples live very lonely lives.

The Anatomy of Separation

When does separation like this in a relationship occur? When you get a divorce or move out? Certainly, this is when separation becomes visible to the rest of the world. Yet, truthfully, separation occurs long before those things happen.

Separation is not a relational tornado that comes out of a clear sky. It is not a surprise attack from an enemy. Separation is more like an ominous hurricane whose swirling winds become stronger and stronger.

Separation is something that occurs over a period of time. It may become apparent to the world when one of you starts living in a hotel, but it starts long before that. Separation occurs when you stop dating. It occurs when you stop eating together on a regular basis and when you cannot find time—or, even worse, make time—to talk. Separation occurs when a wife quits dressing sexy for her husband and when a husband zones out from his wife the moment he gets home from work—and never zones back in.

Separation happens when you quit making love and start making excuses. *We are just too tired... We have been too busy... The kids always need us so we don't have a chance to connect...*

Separation occurs when you no longer battle *for* each other and only battle *with* each other. For some couples, this starts even before they get married. Other couples slide down the path of separation two, five or ten years into marriage. For Ben and Katie in *The Story of Us*, the downward spiral happened this way:

> "Over the years there were less and less moments in the course of the day when Ben and I actually made real eye contact...
>
> "Maybe it was the stuff of life... but after awhile there was a disturbing comfort in not really having to deal with each other because somehow you just get used to the disconnection...
>
> "And, even at night when we could finally come together, we wound up facing forward. Yeah, we were tired, but I think we were afraid that if we faced each other there'd be nothing there."

When their marriage is at the point of divorce, Katie recognizes how they got there. Separation does not happen all of the sudden; it happens in the little things along the way, like avoiding eye contact.

What is the point at which a happy couple, like Ben and Katie, begins to become miserably incompatible? We believe that it is at the point of defensiveness. Separation occurs when you no longer desire to *Align Your Will* in some aspect of your marriage. This is when you are no longer willing to work as a team in one or more areas.

When you and your spouse become perpetually defensive toward each other, you will eventually destroy the trust, communication and passion in your marriage. Ultimately, this defensiveness may kill your desire to be in relationship altogether. Selfishly battling your spouse most definitely does *not* lead to "Fantasy Meets Reality."

The Source of Defensiveness

Whether you are aware of it or not, you have a defense strategy that you use in your marriage. Your spouse does, too. Every person has a defense strategy. This defensiveness comes from hurt, and hurt comes from relationships that have wounded.

From the time you were born, you began to form your defense. All the relationships of your life, and especially your parents' relationship with you and each other, have a lot to do with shaping this defense.

Hurt fractures the lenses of our hearts. Once this occurs—and it does occur for all—we look at every relationship thereafter through these broken lenses. As we look through these, hurt shapes our view of all relationships. We then take this fractured perspective of relationships into our present and future relationships.

So what does this mean? It means that the hurt you experienced from your parents' divorce, your first true love, some painful dating relationships or maybe the demise of your own

Kelly and Tosha Williams

first marriage comes with you into your current marriage. Relationships are cumulative, and so is the hurt. The more hurt you have experienced in relationship, the more likely you are to form thicker walls of defense to protect your heart.

This fractured perspective of relationship shaped by hurt forms our view of how we believe we need to protect ourselves in future relationships (though we do not consciously know we are doing this). Thus, we develop a "defense" to protect ourselves from future relational hurt. This is normal. Everyone does it.

As you enter marriage, you bring these defenses with you. Along the way in marriage, you develop new defenses as you see how your spouse is or is not going to engage you. Your spouse's actions provoke in you reminders of good and bad from past relationships. If you think it is good then there probably will not be a problem. However, if you perceive that your spouse is bringing more hurt into your life, whether it is the same old wound or a new one, you become defensive.

To keep it safe, you begin to hold your heart separate from your spouse.

Defensive Approaches

Unfortunately, you cannot just stop being defensive; you do not have the capacity. Nevertheless, you *do* have the capacity to understand each other's defensiveness and then choose an offensive approach that compliments your spouse's defensiveness at that time.

Everybody has a defensive approach, but the goal in marriage, in order to keep from being separate, is to learn how to *Align Your Will*. This is the antidote to separateness and defensiveness. We believe that this is extremely important, and we want you to hear us very clearly on this: *If you do not Align Your Will to each other, you may stay married, but you will be alone in your marriage.*

In this chapter, we will identify the common ways that couples deal with defensiveness so that you can identify you and your spouse's defensive tendencies. Then, in the next chapter, we will talk about beneficial ways to engage your spouse offensively.

Hopefully, by understanding one another a little better, you will both gain a desire to resolve the issue instead of avoiding it, stuffing it or exploding about it. This will enable you to *Align Your Will*.

So how do you and your spouse approach conflict? Everybody has a defensive way of approaching conflict. Do you know what approach you take when you become defensive?

Some couples deny having conflict in their relationship; other couples have so much conflict that they cannot imagine living any other way. Wherever you are on the conflict spectrum, we are going to unpack three common approaches to conflict. One approach is neither worse nor better than another approach; your defensive approach is not the "right" approach while your spouse's is the "wrong" approach. The following are simply three different ways people defend themselves when there is conflict:

The Surrenderer Approach:
"I don't care whose fault it is. I just want it to be peaceful. I'll give in to you—even if it means me losing—because

peace is so important to me. We need **happiness** in our relationship."

The Fighter Approach:
*"I don't care whose fault it is—though I'm pretty sure it's yours. I am going to fight until we both know who's wrong so we can make some **progress**. We need **honesty** in our relationship."*

The Fleer Approach:
*"I don't know whose fault it is, but I am not going to fight in order to figure it out. I am going to leave this battle and **protect** us both from ourselves. We need **hope** in our relationship."*

What approach is your natural tendency: to surrender, to fight or to flee? What is your spouse's natural tendency?

The Reasons You Are Defensive

To better understand what your approach is, you can try to understand why you take that approach. What motivates you to defend yourself the way you do?

"Surrenderers" take this approach because they do not want anyone to feel defeat. They would rather keep the peace and feel themselves defeated than provoke something in someone else and create conflict that makes others feel defeated. They have had someone make them feel defeated, and they have determined not to be that type of person.

So, if you are a Surrenderer, you often assume the role of defeatist, not because you *are* a defeatist or because you want to lose all the time—winning would be great—but because surrendering brings a feeling of peace to the relationship. You do not like losing any more than anybody else does, but if losing means peace, then you accept peace as your win even if underneath you feel defeat.

"Fighters" take the approach they do because they want to know who is right. Once they decide who is right, they determine whether they should change and how they will change. Of course, Fighters always think they are right going into the battle, but they may eventually conclude that they are wrong depending on how the person they are arguing with engages them or treats them. Ultimately, the Fighter feels self-ordained to lead the quest for truth and find answers.

If you are a Fighter, then you believe that without this pursuit of truth the relationship makes no progress. In your opinion, the relationship will die or drift into a state of numbness without progress. You would rather have chaos, conflict or confusion than silence or avoidance of truth. To you, fighting feels like progress is being made. Unfortunately, deep down, death may still occur in the relationship due to the aggressiveness of your approach and the harsh things you say in the name of progress and truth.

"Fleers" take their approach because they want to protect everyone involved, especially themselves. Their goal is to avoid disappointment. Fleers have learned (or innately assume) that, while surrendering may create disappointment for someone and fighting certainly does, fleeing gives everyone the opportunity to escape disappointment. The Fleer believes that by avoiding the conflict both sides get their space and both parties retain the ability to win. So the

Fleer disengages and runs from the fight, either physically, emotionally or verbally.

If you are a Fleer, then you will run from a conflict in order to win or to make others feel they have won. Being pursued makes you feel valued and protected. However, if you are not pursued, you eventually feel like a loser because you see your flight as the means by which your spouse always wins.

Ultimately, the Surrenderer, the Fighter and the Fleer alike want to feel like winners. How do you know when you have won? Surrenderers know they have won when they feel peace. Fighters know they have won when they feel progress. Fleers know they have won when they feel protected.

How do you know when you have lost? Surrenderers feel like they have lost when they do not feel peace. They may have everything else, but without peace they feel fully defeated.

Fighters feel like they have lost when they do not feel like progress has been made in the relationship. Without some sense of progress, the Fighter feels like nothing else matters in life.

Fleers feel like they have lost when they do not feel protected. Without protection, the Fleer feels disappointed and vulnerable, like they do not matter.

It may seem like Fleers are wimpier in relationship than Fighters. It may appear that Fighters are less self-controlled than Surrenderers. Regardless of what the titles may imply, the fact is that all three of these approaches can be self-centered approaches to a marriage relationship. One is not better or worse than the other.

In the coming pages, we are going to describe three different marriages. The first marriage is "The Fighter versus the Fleer."

The second marriage is "The Surrenderer versus the Fighter."
The third marriage is "The Surrenderer versus the Fleer."

If you have identified your and your spouse's propensities, try inserting your own names into the text as we have done in the first example. Let us see what the defense strategies look like in these three different marriages.

Marriage #1: The Fighter versus the Fleer

Scenario #1: The Fighter Wins

This is our marriage: Kelly is the Fighter, and Tosha is the Fleer. When we have conflict, Kelly wants progress and honesty; Tosha wants protection and hope.

As the Fighter, Kelly wins when he feels he has made progress by establishing the truth about the argument, the situation or the relationship. He bases this truth, of course, on his own opinion, but it nonetheless gives him hope for the future of our relationship. While this is good for Kelly, it is deadly for Tosha because she is the Fleer. In the midst of a Fighter's pursuit of truth, a Fleer does not feel fought *for* but shot *at*. As the Fleer, Tosha feels targeted as the problem that must change, and this feeling provokes in her the desire to sprint. So, she runs while Kelly pursues not her, but the truth, at all costs.

Initially, the Fleer might be glad the Fighter pursues the truth. In time, though, the Fleer often comes to hate the fact that this pursuit is at all costs. Little matters to the Fighter except getting to the bottom of the issue. If the Fleer cannot get away from the Fighter, eventually the Fleer will give up the hope of ever feeling protected by the Fighter.

The Fighter will assume that the Fleer has finally seen the truth the way they see it and that the relationship is making progress. The Fleer will not necessarily see it this way because, truthfully, they will simply have run away to protect themselves.

When Fighters win by fighting for truth in a conflict, Fleers will feel that truth has been used against them. This makes Fleers feel like truth matters more than they do. This eventually builds up resentment toward the Fighter that comes out indirectly in conversations with others where the Fleer feels safe enough to express some honest feelings.

Result #1: As the victor, the Fighter feels the truth has been revealed and progress has been made, while the Fleer feels the Fighter cares more about the truth than about protecting and valuing her in the relationship.

Scenario #2: The Fleer Wins

Fighters often "win" the conflict until Fleers figure out how to control marriage in their own way. As the Fleer, Tosha wins when she is able to protect both of us in a conflict, especially herself. She runs when the environment, the conflict or the argument does not feel safe. What "does not feel safe" is relative to each situation and could be anything from hearing the Fighter use hurtful words to being in a frantic environment.

When a conflict feels precarious, Fleers create whatever is necessary to feel protected and safe. They may go to a different room in the midst of a heated discussion, or they may simply clam up and quit talking. Whatever the means, Fleers try to get away from the hurt, the frustration or the emotions of the battleground.

Unfortunately, over time, protecting themselves like this does not make Fleers feel as valued as they had hoped. Though at first they may not even recognize it, a slow resentment grows because they always have to guard themselves.

For the Fighter, seeing your spouse continually flee from conflict is frustrating. For awhile, the Fighter may pursue the Fleer, but eventually the Fighter will give up because the Fleer just keeps running away from the problems. The Fighter feels exasperated by the Fleer's cowardice in conflict and sees this as a character weakness instead of a protection mechanism. Slowly, this develops an angry, judgmental spirit in the Fighter because the Fleer refuses to see or deal with the truth.

Result #2: Fleers feel safe when they run away and protect themselves, but they may eventually still not feel valued if the Fighters give up pursuing them. On the other hand, the Fighter grows angrier at the Fleer spouse because the Fleer refuses to acknowledge the truth and move the marriage forward.

Marriage #2: The Surrenderer versus the Fighter

Scenario #1: The Surrenderer Wins

Surrenderers win when they feel peace so, many times, a Surrenderer will give up or give in. A Surrenderer might say something like this: "Okay, you're right about me. You're always right; I'm always wrong." This kind of statement is not only an exaggeration, it is not true because nobody is always wrong or always right. Nonetheless, a Surrenderer will portray this attitude in order to end the conflict and bring "peace." Surrender sounds like a noble idea, because you are letting your partner "win." If you always surrender before you make progress, though, you are going to make your spouse feel like death—although you will be happy because you feel peace.

Your Fighter partner will not be able to focus on the peace because truth was not discovered and determined. In the Fighter's mind, no progress was made if no truth about your relationship was uncovered. To the Fighter, peace with no progress is compromise that eventually will destroy your relationship.

Result #1: The Surrenderer feels happy and peaceful while the Fighter feels death and foresees demise in the marriage. The two of you will be polarized about the state of your relationship.

Scenario #2: The Fighter Wins

Fighters have made progress when they have revealed truth based on their terms. Yet, a Fighter who provokes a battle with the Surrenderer spouse makes that person feel defeated. Why? Because fighting does not feel peaceful or happy! While the Fighter sees progress, the Surrenderer feels chaos.

Surrenderers long for peace and happiness. Without this, they feel like they have lost their identity. When they get sucked into a fight, they are forced to become something they are not and do not want to be. Ultimately, when this happens over and over again, Fighters may gain their truth but Surrenderers lose their sense of self. If this is your marriage, this continual loss will drain the vitality from your relationship.

Result #2: The Fighter makes progress and reveals truth while the Surrenderer feels chaotic, defeated and lost. The Fighter spouse wins at the expense of the Surrenderer, which means the marriage loses.

Marriage #3–The Surrenderer versus the Fleer

Scenario #1: The Surrenderer Wins

At initial glance, the marriage between a Surrenderer and a Fleer appears made in heaven. Surrenderers win when they feel peace in the relationship; this peace allows Fleers the comfort of not having to escape since their protection is not threatened. Seems like the perfect marriage, right? This couple may even brag about never arguing.

This may be true, at least superficially. However, just because you do not argue does not mean your marriage is without conflict. Eventually, the avoidance approach will catch up with everybody because even a Surrenderer and a Fleer fight. The problem is, neither partner wants to bring up conflict in order to deal with it. Surrenderers and Fleers feel things as strongly as Fighters, but because they want peace and protection, they often avoid the issues.

Over time, this produces a simmering resentfulness

toward each other. Even though they may never say what they really think or feel, nothing can stay buried forever. Eventually those thoughts and feelings about each other surface either indirectly or maybe even through conversations with others.

When Surrenderers win by keeping the peace at all costs, Fleers do not feel fought for and, thus, not protected by Surrenderers. This lack of overt protection leaves Fleers feeling disappointed, like they do not matter to the Surrenderers. Fleers then retreat because they do not need peace; they need protection. They need to be fought for even when Surrenderers cannot find it within to fight.

Result #1: Both parties initially feel peace—especially the Surrenderer—but the Fleer eventually does not feel fought for or protected which makes that person feel like he does not matter.

Scenario #2: The Fleer Wins

Fleers win when they feel protected, and they will do anything they can to reduce their vulnerability. If Fleers do not feel protected, then they will protect themselves by running away from the conflict. Fleers may run away physically, emotionally or verbally. Whatever their tactic, Fleers will go somewhere else so that they are no longer vulnerable.

The problem is that, as we have discussed throughout the book, vulnerability is an essential key to REAL marriage. When a Fleer runs away and deliberately chooses not to be vulnerable, she hinders her relationship with her Surrender.

In addition, the Fleer's absence will make the Surrenderer

spouse feel chaotic and insecure. This creates a panic in the Surrenderer, who most likely will pursue the Fleer in order to restore peace. The Fleer then feels protected by the Surrenderer. The Surrenderer, too, feels peace again. Over the years, however, resentment grows from this interplay because the Surrenderer feels defeated because the Fleer always wins at all cost.

Result #2: The Fleer feels protected but resentment begins to grow in the Surrenderer because of always having to pursue the Fleer. Their marriage is stifled through lack of vulnerability.

Separation Hurts

In *The Story of Us*, Ben and Katie act as if everything is just fine when they put their two children on the bus headed for summer camp. As soon as their kids are gone, though, so are their smiles. The two are on the defensive in their marriage. They are separate to their cores, fighting against each other. When the kids leave for a few weeks, Ben and Katie get as far away from each other as they can.

Maybe the two of you are not physically separated; maybe you are emotionally or sexually separated. Maybe you are one of those couples who sent out the smiling Christmas card this past year. In your heart of hearts, you know that you are not as happy as the picture portrays.

Perhaps you show up at parties together, go to school functions together, even attend church together, but you live as two very different people in private. Maybe, like us, you had a huge fight last night right before company rang the doorbell. Then you had to put on your happy faces and act as if everything were fine.

Short separations, long separations, they all hurt a relationship. Are you and your spouse separate from each other, physically, emotionally, sexually, spiritually? If you are, it is possibly because you have quit being willing to *Align Your Will* to one another. Maybe you have never attempted to *Align Your Will* to one another because you never learned how.

In the next chapter, we are going to talk about how to move from your natural, selfish defensive approach in conflict to a selfless, offensive approach. An offensive approach is one which enables you to step back and recognize what your spouse needs from you during a conflict. If, after reading this chapter, you are still unclear about the three approaches to conflict, we encourage you to keep reading. While this chapter looked at the approaches from a negative angle, the next chapter explains them from a positive view. Understanding how to bless your spouse through an offensive approach to conflict may help you better realize who you are or who you want to be.

Engaging conflict with an offensive approach is the way you begin to *Align Your Will* with one another. This is what creates an opportunity for REAL marriage to flourish.

Come on, Surrenderers, Fighters and Fleers. Let's figure out how to be in REAL marriage with each other as we lay down our personal defense strategies and employ the offensive method in the midst of conflict.

For Discussion:

1.   What do you do when there is a conflict between you and

your spouse? Do you leave the room? Do you give up? Do you yell louder? What does this tell you about your defensive approach? Are you a Fleer, Surrenderer or Fighter? You may see yourself as a combination of these. Which is your main approach? Secondary?

2. Did you and your spouse disagree on the approach you think you take? If so, as a Surrenderer, you will want to change your answer to keep the peace. As a Fighter, you will be determined to fight about it to find out who is right so you can make progress in the relationship. As a Fleer, you will try to avoid answering this question, and you may even want to stop reading this book altogether right now because it does not feel safe. What emotions are provoked in you right now?

3. Maybe you are still having a hard time identifying your natural defensive approach. Think about what you most desire when you and your spouse have conflict. Which one of the following motifs is the *most* important to you:
    • Peace (everyone is happy)–You want to figure out how to mediate conflict.
    • Progress (the truth is revealed)–You are somewhat excited about conflict.
    • Protection (everyone is safe)–You want to escape conflict.

4. When you do not achieve what you so desire in a conflict, which of the following is your first natural reaction? When you feel this way, how does this play itself out in your marriage?
    • Defeat (something was lost)

- Death (nothing else matters)
- Disappointment (you don't matter)

11. the offensive

"You love who we were. You couldn't possibly love what we've become... We can't stay together just because we get a glimpse of us every once in awhile."
— *Katie in* The Story of Us

"I thought you two said you weren't going to fight this year!" Our third grade daughter thought she had us this time, as she added her sideline analysis to our battle.

Neither of us could remember this commitment amongst our past New Year's resolutions. However, maybe we *should* have made a pledge not to fight because here we were at it again, fighting over something that did not even really matter.

We love each other, and we are very committed to our marriage. There are seasons, though, when we exhaust one another with fighting our battles.

What about you? Are you tired of fighting? Are you

weary from the conflict? If you are, then we invite you to consider a new approach for your marriage. Instead of using a defensive approach to conflict, the two of you can employ an offensive approach.

A New Approach

You started moving to a new rhythm in your marriage with *Realizing the Cost* and *Embracing Spiritual Guideposts*. Now you begin to *Align Your Will* to your spouse in a very practical way.

You should know that, if you are going to *Align Your Will* and experience REAL marriage in the midst of conflict, then you will be required to work together as a couple. To do this, you have to make a shift from fighting *against* each other to battling *for* each other. In conflict, the distinction between these two prepositions makes all the difference. When you *Align Your Will,* you learn to battle *for* your relationship instead of *against* it.

In battling *for* each other, we are not elevating the Fighter's approach from the last chapter. The Fighter enters conflict the way he does for selfish reasons. Conversely, when you both—no matter whether you are naturally a Surrenderer, Fighter or Fleer—battle *for* the other person, you will go about your relationship in a selfless manner.

How do you do this? How do you stop fighting *with* each other and start battling *for* each other? Battling *for* each other seems impossible when you are at odds with one another. So what do you do? Sulk, scream and separate or submit and sacrifice? These latter two are dirty terms in our culture, but they have the ability to bring REAL marriage together in ways that the former can never do. Fantasy can meet reality in your marriage only as you and your spouse are vulnerable enough to submit to one another's needs and sacrifice for each other.

If we are going to lay down the weapons of defensiveness and take up the tools of an offensive approach to marriage, then we must begin with a challenge Jesus gave in the first century. He said:

> If any of you wants to be My follower, you must turn from your selfish ways, take up your cross, and follow Me.
>
> Mark 8:34

While at initial reading this has nothing to do with marriage, it has everything to do with battling for someone other than yourself. We believe this is what marriage is all about.

Being Selfless

How do you "turn from your selfish ways" and fight *for* your spouse in marriage? What we want to suggest seems contrary to common sense, the opposite of logic. Still, fighting *for* your spouse makes all the difference in the offensive approach to the battles in marriage.

When a conflict comes into your marriage, begin to ask yourself this question, "What does my spouse need in this argument right now?" Determine to lay down your natural weapon of defense, be that to fight, surrender or flee. Focus on your spouse. Being spouse-focused rather than self-centered will make a huge difference in your marriage.

Focusing on what your spouse needs in a conflict means laying down your preconceived notions of how a conflict should go. It means taking a new approach that probably will not feel comfortable and certainly will not be easy. Focusing on your spouse's needs means being concerned about someone other than yourself.

This may be easy to do when you are not in a conflict; it is painfully difficult when you are in the midst of an argument. Yet, this is where a positive offensive approach begins.

You start with knowing what your own tendency in conflict is: Fighter, Surrenderer or Fleer. As we discussed in the last chapter, do you most desire progress, peace or protection? With this understanding about yourself, ask yourself what your spouse needs from you. Does your spouse need progress, peace or protection right now? Since your spouse most likely needs something different than you, this informs you how to "turn from your selfish ways" toward your spouse and your marriage.

You might say, "How am I supposed to know what my spouse needs?" Begin with what you know about your spouse. From the last chapter, recall how your husband identified himself or how your wife classified herself. Is your spouse a Surrenderer, a Fighter or a Fleer?

If your partner is a Surrenderer, then you know that he values peace above all and desperately desires the feeling of happiness in your marriage. If your spouse is a Fighter, then you realize she most values progress in your relationship and sees honesty as the way to achieve that. If your spouse is a Fleer, then you understand he values protection above all and sincerely hopes for better days in your marriage.

Kelly and Tosha Williams

When you fight *for* your spouse, you will realize in the back of your mind that your spouse is most likely one of these three styles (or, at least, tends to be one way more than the others). Be sensitive to this fact. Learn your spouse's battle techniques and use those on her behalf in conflict. If you are in the midst of marital war, doing this may seem like using your enemy's weapons against them. This may be true. Nonetheless, by using your spouse's conflict techniques on his behalf, you will begin battling for that person, maybe for the first time.

The following scenarios illustrate how you can be selfless and put your spouse's needs above your own. As in the last chapter, we will start with the marriage scenario that best describes us as a couple. Again, we will insert our names in a few places just as we encourage you to do in the scenario that best illustrates your marriage. These are examples of how you can battle *for* your spouse.

Marriage #1: The Fighter versus the Fleer

Scenario #1: You are the Fighter. In conflict, how do you selflessly love your Fleer?

When we have conflict, Kelly wants to fight and Tosha wants to flee. Kelly wants progress and honesty; Tosha wants protection and hope. When we argue, Kelly can bring both honesty and hope at the same time by being honest about his own hurt.

This goes against a Fighter's natural tendency, though. Fighters tend to be angry people. It is not like they always kick the cat, but when something goes wrong, anger is their first natural reaction. It is powerfully important that Fighters learn how to express their *hurt* instead of their *anger*.

If you are a Fighter, you must deny your desire to be angry and, instead, seek to create a feeling of protection for your Fleer. Don't assume the Fleer wants to be left alone; that could not be further from the truth. The Fleer does not want you to yell, accuse or leave her unprotected. Your Fleer wants to feel like you want to protect her more than win a fight against her.

As you make protection the priority over fighting, your Fleer will become more open to your pursuit. As you pursue your spouse, two things will happen. You will be able to control your own feelings, and you will draw out your Fleer's honest hurt. This will reveal a vulnerable side of your spouse that may often be smothered in the heat of the battle. You may be surprised that the Fleer's vulnerability will soften your own heart and help you recognize the emotions other than anger that you have. You will feel your own brokenness and begin to need protection in the relationship, just like your spouse does. This will put the two of you on equal ground.

In addition, as you understand your own brokenness, you will start to see why you get so angry about certain things toward your spouse. You will start to see that not everything is entirely your spouse's fault. You have pain in your life, too. This perspective gives you the opportunity to learn how to share your hurt with your spouse instead of spew your anger.

Result #1: When you, the Fighter, lay aside the fight in order to pursue your Fleer, you will help your spouse feel protected while finding safety yourself in which to address your own brokenness.

Scenario #2: You are the Fleer. In conflict, how do you selflessly love your Fighter?

If you are a Fleer, it is time to fight. If you spend your whole life protecting yourself, you will destroy your spouse in the end. Why? Because your Fighter spouse will eventually give up. At first, that may sound like a good thing because the raging force against you will subside. However, as much as you dislike the fight, you will find that some of the essence of your spouse dies when that spark that makes him a Fighter is extinguished.

You may think this could never happen. You may think that your Fighter will always be willing to fight, but that is not the case. Fighters are not marathon conflict resolvers; they are sprinters. They want to resolve conflict quickly most of the time.

You, on the other hand, always feel there is time to resolve. You may assume your Fighter will be ready to fight whenever you are finally ready to engage the conflict. However, this assumption will get you in trouble because, one day, this will all change, maybe without warning. The Fighter will finally take your tactic and give up or run away in your relationship just like you do.

Do not let your marriage go down this path. If you are a Fleer, you must deny your desire to escape. You must be honest about why you want to run away. You have to quit controlling every conflict by leaving it. Sometimes you must stay put and fight for your marriage.

The next time you have a conflict, do not immediately run away from the anger you feel vented at you. Give your Fighter the chance to get past the initial angry emotions and to express the real reasons behind the conflict. Let your wife speak into your desire to control everything by fleeing. Give your husband the chance to express how your selfish control has hurt him.

When you, the Fleer, take responsibility for how you have tried to control the marriage through fleeing, this honesty will give your Fighter the sense of progress. Your Fighter will feel valued when you are willing to quit running away so that your relationship can move ahead.

Result #2: As the Fleer, when you refrain from running away in conflict, your Fighter will feel progress in your relationship and you will confront your own selfishness control through wanting to flee.

Marriage #2: The Surrenderer versus the Fighter

Scenario #1: You are the Surrenderer. In conflict, how do you selflessly love your Fighter?

If you are the Surrenderer, you must force yourself to engage the battle for your Fighter. As much as it goes against your natural tendencies, as much as it will pain you, you must force yourself to fight.

You might be thinking, "Why in the world would I want to do this? It's ridiculous!" Yes, telling you "to fight" outside the proper context would be ridiculous. However, your

Fighter needs you to deny your desire for peace and to fight for the truth and progress that will help your marriage.

What does this look like? How do you fight as a Surrenderer? First, you must accept the fact that your spouse is probably a better arguer than you are (most Fighters are compared to Surrenderers and Fleers). Nonetheless, you must still go there, into the fight with your Fighter. You must not try to keep the peace at all costs. You cannot simply pretend that everything is okay. You must allow your spouse to be honest—and you must be honest, too. You have to allow your spouse to confess her true feelings, and you do the same.

This will make your Fighter feel like progress is happening, and this progress makes your Fighter spouse feel *fought for*. This will give the Fighter a sense of truth and honesty.

This honesty will expose you to the fact that peace has been your way of selfishly controlling the marriage. The peace you feel is not true peace when you surrender just for the sake of peace. This is false peace because it is selfish peace. It is your way of controlling your marriage and your spouse; it keeps your partner at a safe distance from you.

If you will engage the fight for truth with your Fighter spouse, you will begin to make progress because you will see how you have wounded your spouse. Controlling the marriage, even when you achieve peace, is very hurtful to the partner who is made to feel like all he wants to do is fight. Honesty exposes your self-centered control through peace.

Though it is painful, this revelation shows you what hinders your ability to love your spouse well. Instead of immediately surrendering as soon as conflict arises, give your Fighter the chance to vent her feelings, emotions, desires or needs.

This honesty gives the Fighter the freedom to say certain things to you that he otherwise would never be able to because normally you use peace to keep from hearing the painful truth. Through hearing the truth, you have the opportunity to own it. Owning the truth releases you from the conflict and allows you to do something about it, like change, apologize, forgive or simply encourage. This will be a circuitous route, but it will take your relationship to the peace—the true peace—you so desperately desire.

Result #1: As the Surrenderer, when you intentionally postpone peace, you give your Fighter the opportunity to feel progress is made in the marriage while you are able to own truth about yourself.

Scenario #2: You are the Fighter. In conflict, how do you selflessly love your Surrenderer?

Everything in you is going to want to fight, but you must stop yourself from going there. It is easy for you to sense that you have hurt your Surrenderer and then focus on building an argument against that person. A Fighter often does this as a defense mechanism, but in doing so the Fighter further destroys the Surrenderer spouse.

Instead, as the Fighter, you must begin to focus less on winning and more on creating an environment of peace. You can do this the same way your Surrenderer spouse does it every day for you. First, you have to postpone the conflict. Avoiding conflict is the very thing you fear, so you will have to force yourself to postpone it.

You must also learn how to keep the peace. You can do

this by learning how to ask your spouse if you can discuss something rather than confronting her, saying she did wrong and then diving into a fight. To avoid fighting or at least to postpone conflict, you need to think about what your spouse needs rather than what he or she has done wrong. Try to fulfill that need you have identified instead of insisting on what your spouse has done wrong.

When you *do* address the conflict, you must pursue peace as much as your Surrenderer does. This will take all the emotion out of the fight for you, but it is what the Surrenderer needs so the situation feels peaceful instead of chaotic and destructive.

Surrendering is no easy task for a Fighter. Yet, surrender is how you "turn from your selfish ways" in a conflict if you are a Fighter married to a Surrenderer. Denying yourself by stopping the fight will expose your own fears. It will reveal the lies you have bought about yourself, your spouse, the marriage you share and the world you occupy.

As you recognize the fears of your heart, you may find your perspective about your Surrenderer spouse begins to change. Up to this point, you may have seen your Surrenderer spouse as the fearful one in the relationship. Through this denying-of-yourself process, you will discover as a Fighter the fears you were covering up through your explosive approach to arguing. This will free you to feel your fears and wrestle with them independently of your struggles with your spouse. As a result, you will progress not only in your marriage but also in who you are as a person.

Result #2: If you, the Fighter, will lay aside the conflict in order to seek peace, your Surrenderer will receive the gift of peace while the truth of your own heart will be revealed.

Marriage #3: The Surrenderer versus the Fleer

Scenario #1: You are the Surrenderer. In conflict, how do you selflessly love your Fleer?

These are the couples of whom it is said after fifty years of marriage, "They never argued." Of course, the reason they do not argue is because one runs away while the other gives up. Once there is an unavoidable conflict, though, a time bomb goes off. Your conflict strategy may not be arguing, but you will have conflict.

How do you, the Surrenderer, selflessly work through conflict for your Fleer? Remember, you want peace, and your spouse wants protection. So, first, you have to acknowledge that peace and protection are not the same thing. Peace for the sake of peace alone only creates an illusion of protection.

Surrenderers work equally hard to keep the peace with everyone, not just their spouses. Eventually, though, there will be relationships and situations that make the Surrenderers choose with whom they will keep the peace. For example, there will come a point when a Surrenderer cannot please both her parents and her husband, or when another Surrenderer cannot make both his friends and his wife happy. When conflicts like these arise, Surrenderers often make a choice that they expect Fleers to "understand."

When this happens in your life, your Fleer will not always simply understand; that person may run away instead. This will create chaos for both of you. Your once harmonious relationship will now feel like a minefield. Who will budge? If you are the Surrenderer and you are going to be selfless, then *you* must learn to budge. You must learn to deny your peace in order to protect your Fleer spouse.

This may require you to engage conflict by pursuing your Fleer, and this will not be easy for you. You will be going out on a dangerous limb, a place that does not feel peaceful at all. But your Fleer will feel protected by your pursuit. This is selfless because you will meet your spouse's needs while you turn your back on what you need.

You have always avoided conflict in order to protect yourself from feeling more hurt in your own heart. As you selflessly pursue your spouse, you will feel vulnerable, the very thing you have tried to avoid because vulnerability brings up too much pain. Still, it is good for you to experience vulnerability and to feel the pain in your own life because this will give you sympathy to care for the pain of your Fleer. Moreover, vulnerability forces you to look at your own heart with greater honesty.

Your Fleer will observe your transformation from a distance and may internally process your sacrifice. Eventually, as the safety and protection factor in the relationship increases, the resentment between the two of you can decrease. This can bring your Fleer out of the foxhole and back into the relationship.

As the Fleer comes back into the relationship through your denial of peace and desire to protect, the Fleer will feel the freedom to be vulnerable in new ways. The sacrifice and humility you have demonstrated gives the Fleer the freedom from being defensive. This enables both of you to face the hurt in your hearts instead of avoiding it through false peace or false protection. Moreover, this will bring hope into your marriage, and you will begin communicating in ways you have never before experienced.

Result #1: When you, the Surrenderer, lay aside your primary desire for peace in order for your Fleer spouse to feel protected, you will begin to face the hurt in your own heart, something you must do before you can experience true peace.

Scenario #2: You are the Fleer. In conflict, how do you selflessly love your Surrenderer?

As the Fleer, you want protection. Your Surrenderer spouse, on the other hand, wants peace. When conflict goes like normal between the two of you, you can stay in the presence of your Surrenderer spouse because that person is reliable for keeping the peace. The Surrenderer will consistently do everything possible to make things seem okay.

Unfortunately, this is a time bomb for your relationship. Eventually something will happen to lose the peace. Then you as the Fleer will have to choose *not* to run away, not to sleep on the couch, not to go to your parent's house.

Choosing not to flee will make you feel unprotected and, thus, vulnerable. You may have spent all your life running from your true feelings, so everything in you will want to escape. Running away feels safer than staying put in conflict. As the Fleer, you must intentionally choose to be vulnerable. This vulnerability will bring up fears that are difficult to face. It will cause you to feel fear as you have never felt it before.

Fleers tend to be very fearful people when conflict arises,

so you try to get away from it quickly. This is your way to control both your emotions and the situation at hand. Consider what you achieve through your control, though. Your avoidance of the conflict makes your Surrenderer feel turmoil because you have removed yourself from the situation. This makes your spouse feel very unsafe.

This will cause the Surrenderer to do what she always does: try to make peace quickly. You must not allow your Surrenderer to do this, though. You must engage your spouse and address the conflict by being vulnerable about your *own* fears.

You must say things like, "I left because I was afraid of..." and then describe what you perceived would happen. To deny yourself in conflict, you must also say to your Surrenderer, "I want you to feel peaceful, so what can I do to help make that happen?"

Your humility will give your spouse a sense of peace, which will enable him to address how he feels about you or the conflict. This gives the Surrenderer a safe place to share hurt while trusting that peace will not leave.

The moment peace leaves is the moment the Surrenderer stops sharing. You can maintain peace by not being defensive and by, instead, allowing your Surrenderer to speak. Let yourself feel the full effect of your spouse's fears. Because you are a Fleer, everything in you will want to run and hide, but don't.

As the Surrenderer shares and you listen, she will slowly get the impression that it is okay to be vulnerable about hurt. As the Surrenderer shares, you will find freedom to feel your own fear. You will begin to understand the lies you have bought about yourself. One example of this might be the rationalization that when conflict arises you have to protect yourself because nobody else will.

In REAL marriage, that is not true. Your spouse—be that person a Surrenderer, Fighter or Fleer—wants to fight for you. Facing your own fears and need for protection will help you love your spouse better in future conflict. Furthermore, as you address your fears, the Surrenderer will feel safe and peaceful to share his own hurts.

Result #2: As the Fleer, laying down your need for protection will give your Surrenderer the greatest opportunity to feel peace. In that peaceful environment together, you will be able to confront your own fears with your spouse instead of trying to protect yourself all by yourself.

Living the Offensive Approach

When the two of us are in the midst of a conflict, the last thing either of us wants to do is to be selfless. There are days when we look at each other during an argument and wonder how in the world we will ever get past the situation at hand. Nobody, us included, is perfect at implementing the offensive approach for one another.

It is helpful for each of us to remember that the real enemy is not the other person. It is *self.* If *I* must win, then self wins. On the other hand, if we want our relationship to win, then self cannot be our primary focus.

This is why you must "turn from your selfish ways." Initially, this feels painful and emotionally bloody, but self-lessness is the best strategy to battle *for* your spouse instead of *against* that person.

Kelly and Tosha Williams

In the next chapter, we will look at how you can know if your marriage is winning when you battle for each other. You are already learning how to "turn from your selfish ways" in conflict; you do this by living the offensive approach of battling *for* your spouse. Now, let us look at how to "take up your cross" in marriage. Believe it or not, taking up your cross in marriage has a lot to do with what victories you will experience in the battlegrounds of life.

As your REAL marriage experiences victories, you will find that "Fantasy Meets Reality" like never before.

Discussion Questions:

We encourage you not to wait until you are in a conflict before you go through the following questions! Now is the time to figure out how best to fight *for* your spouse and marriage. Plan a date for sometime soon to figure out your marriage's offensive strategy.

1. Which offensive approaches best describe each of you? Which scenario best illustrates your marriage? Why?

2. Even the scenario that best describes your marriage does not perfectly describe it. What is different for you and your spouse in conflict than what is described in the stereotype? Discuss this together.

3. Make an intentional decision not to get angry at each other, then talk through a major conflict your marriage has faced in the past. Using the offensive strategies from this chapter, discuss how each of you could have handled that situation in a more pro-active way. Analyze that conflict in order

to understand better how to handle other conflicts in the future. Allow each other the freedom to say, "This is what I needed from you," or "This is how you might have handled that better." Do not let negative emotions steal the power of this discussion, because it can teach you how to battle *for* each other instead of *against* each other.

4. How will you better implement an offensive approach for each other in the future?

5. After you have employed your offensive approach for a while—and have experienced it through a few conflicts—plan another date. Discuss whether your new approach is helping your marriage communication. Talk about whether you are going through conflict in a more healthy way. If you have not seen any improvements, you may want to seek some help from a friend or professional. If you have seen some positive changes, then celebrate!

12. the victory

"I've always felt that no matter what Katie and I were going through, no matter how painful things got, if our feet found each other under the blankets—even just the slightest connection—it would let us know that we'd entered the de-militarized zone, that we were going to be okay, that we were still an us."

–Ben in The Story of Us

Everybody likes to be a winner. Watch how a woman responds when she wins the door prize or how a man reacts when he wins the office pool. We all like to feel the glory of victory, no matter how big or small that success may be.

Though you may have never thought about your marriage in these terms, we bet you want to experience a winning marriage. You want to feel the elation of victory in this relationship to which you have committed your life.

What does it mean to experience victory in your REAL marriage? How do you know if your marriage is winning or not? It is easy to know if you personally are winning based on how *you* feel about the marriage. But, how do you know if your marriage is winning from your spouse's perspective? How do you know if you are truly finding each other under the covers of life after all your years together?

We believe your marriage is winning when you have a connection in every area of your relationship. This happens as each of you *Align Your Will* to one another.

Your Marriage Cross

In the last chapter, we discussed "turning from your selfish ways." This is your offensive approach to conflict, your strategy for battling for your spouse. By being selfless, you are setting up your marriage for a win (though it may not feel that way initially). This is a lifelong process, but a winning marriage does not stop there.

The next step of a winning marriage is to "take up your cross." As quoted in the last chapter, Jesus said:

> If any of you wants to be My follower, you must turn from your selfish ways, take up your cross, and follow Me.
>
> Mark 8:34

For Jesus, the cross symbolized the burdens He carried on behalf of others. Your cross in marriage is the burden you carry on behalf of your spouse. It is how you bail water, as we discussed in chapter four. It is part of an offensive strategy, as we discussed in chapter eleven. It is what you do to make your marriage successful.

This may seem like upside down logic. It may not make sense how burdens are a good thing. Nevertheless, when you both bear burdens for each other and your marriage, you will discover success like never before in your marriage.

How do you do this in marriage? You sacrifice for your spouse by helping that person along life's way. In REAL marriage, you carry burdens for each other.

There are burdens that you carry in every realm of your life. Some burdens are very evident since your spouse obviously needs your help. Other burdens are not so obvious because they are buried under layers of hurt and pain.

As you read the following pages, begin to ask yourself, what burdens do I carry for my spouse and what burdens do I *need* to carry for my spouse? The answers you discover are vital for REAL marriage. By carrying burdens for your spouse, you are taking up the cross of marriage.

As you read the coming pages, also think about the burdens that your spouse carries for you. What sacrifices does your spouse make on your behalf? Furthermore, what burdens do you need your spouse to carry for you?

Then we encourage you to take this thought process a step further. After each of you processes this chapter individually, you need to process it as a couple. Instead of waiting until you are in a fight to spew "Look at everything I do for you" at your spouse, make a special time to talk about the sacrifices each of you makes along the way.

Talking with each other about the burdens you carry is not bragging. It is a vital step toward communication in your marriage. It is more than okay to talk about this; it is beneficial to hold up what you do and say, "This is how I help our marriage and family function better."

Likewise, it is important to communicate with your spouse the areas where you need help. Do not wait until you are in the midst of a conflict or struggle to express this; do it along life's way.

Your marriage experiences REAL victory when the two of you can honestly look at the needs of your relationship and carry the burdens together. You did not marry to experience life alone. You got married to experience connection with the person you fell in love with. "Fantasy Meets Reality" is all about the great parts of life intersecting with the difficult areas. Those difficult areas are the burdens that you may need to bear for your spouse. Here are some to consider.

Emotional Burdens

We all wrestle with things in life and, usually, this pain begins to affect us emotionally. Whether it is a bad day at work, a hard night with the children or a painful meeting with a friend, our emotions are affected. Physical sickness usually leads to emotional sickness. Financial issues often lead to emotional despair. Relational problems regularly make us depressed. It seems like just about every aspect of life eventually affects us in our emotions.

Some people wrestle with severe emotional struggles for which medication is required. Other people struggle with undiagnosed issues. In the emotional realm, there are many, many possibilities.

Ask your spouse what long-term emotional burdens he bears for you, and then listen. Let your wife share with you the burdens she bears on your behalf. You may be surprised to learn some things about yourself that you did not know. You may not even realize the ways that your spouse makes your life easier. You may also hear some things you need to change.

After your husband expresses the burdens he bears for you, then turn the tables by asking what burdens he needs you to bear for him. Ask your wife how you can better help her in this area. If your spouse does not know the answer to this question, then you should give some suggestions. (Surely this will score you some points!)

Spiritual Burdens

As we discussed in chapters six and seven, you are a spiritual being with spiritual needs. Although some marriages are very spiritual, you and your spouse may not be into spirituality. If you avoid this realm, we think you are missing out on a lot of connection and beauty. As you read in previous chapters, we believe that God wants to be involved in your marriage.

For us, the foundation of our relationship is spiritual. In our marriage, we individually use prayer and the Ancient Scriptures, along with church participation, as a way to incorporate spirituality into our lives. For the sake of our relationship, though, we also have a weekly time when we pray together and share our hearts with one another. There is no greater time of gratification for our marriage than when we pray for each other.

Even though I am a pastor, I often find it easiest to pray

with Tosha after we have turned out the lights and gone to bed. This may sound ironic, since I speak and even pray in front of hundreds of people every week. When I am being truly vulnerable, though, sometimes it takes a darkened bedroom for me to feel safe. I love resting beside Tosha in bed and sharing my heart through prayer. Many nights, tears have streamed down my cheeks during this sacred time.

Ask your wife how she would like for you to be more intentional about your spiritual relationship. Talk to your husband about how he desires for you to invest in him spiritually. If you have never had a prayer time together or read the Ancient Scriptures together, take the opportunity to do so. Bonding spiritually can be another of the "thousand strands" that connect your marriage.

Sexual Burdens

For the average couple, there is the normal question of how often you should have sex each week. You may want to have it more—or less—than your spouse does. Most men want to have sex every day, every other day or at least every few days; most wives are content with quite a bit less than that. For other couples, the wife has the driving libido while the husband does not.

You bear a burden in your marriage when you sacrifice for your spouse sexually, meeting that person's needs and desires. We are not talking about being a slave; we are talking about being your spouse's partner in sexuality instead of having a semi-regular headache. The sexual aspect of marriage is what sets marriage apart from all other relationships. Though men often desire it more often than women, women are still sexual beings in need of connection. You may want it less than your spouse; you may want it more than your spouse. Either way, you will have to sacrifice for your marriage to experience victory in this area.

Like most men, I like to have sex at least three times a week. I also like to explore other creativity in our sexual experience. Over the years, Tosha has been willing to take these risks on my behalf. That means tons to me, and I try in other areas of our marriage to show my appreciation for these sacrifices she makes for me.

Now is the tell-tale time for your marriage. Ask your spouse, "What burdens do you bear for me in the sexual realm?" Listen; don't get defensive. Then ask, "What burdens do you want me to bear for you in the sexual realm?" Husband, you may hear your wife say that she wants you to connect with her more emotionally. Wife, you may hear your husband ask you if you would be willing to do it tonight.

If you really want "Fantasy Meets Reality" in your marriage, you cannot—you must not—neglect the sexual burdens that your spouse wants you and needs you to bear. In the last section of the book, we will talk more about how to make this less of a "burden" and more of a "new experience." Who knows? You may be surprised that this "burden" becomes more fulfilling and pleasurable than you ever imagined!

Time Burdens

Some couples, after being married for a while, begin to neglect spending intentional time together. They are married, but they live together as roommates functioning independently of one another. This is not a marriage; it is an arrangement. Where there is an arrangement, eventually there is no marriage.

Your soul needs time to connect with your spouse; your spouse needs time to connect with you. Unfortunately, you may not be in the mood when your spouse is. How often does your spouse want to spend time together but you do not want to? How often do you bear the burden of spending time with your spouse when you want to do something else that appeases your selfishness? For the wife, that time may be when your husband wants to have sex but you are hoping to finish a project. For the husband, that time may be when your wife wants to talk and you want to play *PlayStation*.

Ask your spouse about the time you spend alone and together. What burdens do you carry for each other? What burdens should you carry? Listen to what your partner has to say; don't be defensive. Start doing whatever your spouse asks at least one time a week. You will be amazed at the change.

Burdens of Past Abuse

Your spouse may have been abused at some point in life. This history may wreak physical havoc on your husband or emotional chaos on your wife. You may not want to have to deal with this burden on a daily basis, but that choice is not yours to make. Whatever neglect, abuse or destructive measures were directed at your spouse, have also been, in a way, directed at you, too. You bear the burden of past abuse when you enter into your spouse's pain and care about how your actions affect this area.

We find that most couples in the first five years of marriage stay away from this issue. However, as time goes on, the pain of the past leaks into marriage and, especially, into conflict resolution. Many of the fears people have in conflict are born out of pain from the past. Hurt from the past crucially shapes their personal defense strategies.

If your spouse struggles with the pain of past abuse, you will bless your spouse by recognizing this and remembering it during conflict. One spark in this battleground may be that of displaced emotion as your spouse vents upon you the negative emotions caused by someone else. There may be times when you have to look beyond the hurt your wife is causing you as a result of the hurt she endured earlier in life. You may have to offer your husband extra love, patience and forgiveness when he attacks you because of the attacks he endured.

We are *not* suggesting that you allow yourself to be abused so that the cycle of abuse repeats. We are simply saying that, in REAL marriage, you must battle offensively for your spouse when you are in this battleground and the sparks begin to fly.

See your spouse's pain for what it is, and bear this burden for him or her. If this burden is too heavy, do not try to bear it alone. Seek professional help if you must or, at least, find support within a caring community of people.

Vocational Burdens

Whether you live your marriage by the traditional vocational model (husband works away and the wife works in the home), by a more contemporary model (where you both work for a paycheck) or by some unusual model you have created, there are burdens that each of you must bear vocationally. It is important that you identify what these are so that you can best support each other in this area.

Whatever the vocational model in your marriage, you each have to sacrifice with and for each other. Career goals, personal aspirations and educational objectives may have to be placed aside for the sake of the greater good in your relationship. When kids come along, even more sacrifices are required.

You may work an uninspiring, dead-end job solely for the sake of providing for your family. Or your spouse may have to work long hours away from home so you have to pick up the slack around the house and carry all the domestic responsibilities. Whether you get a paycheck or not, the work you do to keep your marriage and family afloat is your vocational burden.

Ask your wife what vocational burdens she carries for you and what vocational burdens she needs you to carry for her. Ask your husband the same questions. If your marriage is being irreversibly damaged by your jobs, either change vocations or change your vocational model. On the other hand, thank one another for the roles you play in each other's lives.

Financial Burdens

Seldom do two people marry and enter marriage with the same model of finances. Often one is a saver while one is a spender. Sometimes one is okay with debt but the other is not. In other relationships, one partner lived off a budget growing up while the other spent freely.

Many people today enter marriage with a lot of debt. Other people have spending problems. Still other people are very controlling about how the finances ought to be spent.

Finances are not an easy burden to bear for one another. This could very well be the biggest category of conflict in your marriage. Financial differences create incredible tensions in relationship, especially when money gets tight or dreams go unrealized because of debt.

Ask your husband what financial burdens he must carry for you. Give your wife the chance to articulate how she compensates for your financial weaknesses. Maybe you are—can you admit it?—irresponsible with your family's finances. Perhaps you are too controlling with them. After a fight breaks out (we are betting that one will!) and you have another chance to practice the offensive strategies of chapter eleven, then move ahead by asking your partner what burdens you need to carry financially in your marriage.

This may very well involve multiple discussions about a budget, spending, saving and debt. If you cannot work through finances without a bomb exploding, you may want to seek professional financial assistance.

Relational Burdens

Obviously, each of you has relationships with other people. Unfortunately, you may not care for your spouse's friends, or your spouse may not like yours. Do you maintain a friendship or bag it when it brings conflict into your marriage?

Other marriages face different relational issues. A wife dreams that her husband would get a few friends. A husband longs for his wife to be more hospitable. You marry somebody then discover that person is not as relational as you would like or is too relational. What do you do?

Somewhere along the way, you have to give your spouse freedom in the relational realm. Your burden may be accepting the fact that your spouse is a true introvert and does not need many relationships to feel content. The burden you may need to carry is to allow more people into your relational circle. Or you may need to tolerate some friendships that your spouse already has.

Relational burdens are often very challenging to navigate. We certainly do not know all the answers, but we do have some suggestions in this area. Look for ways that you can each be with your friends on a somewhat consistent basis. Do not make your marriage a prison that prevents either of you from having other relationships. On the other hand, do not force your friends upon your spouse. We made this mistake early in our marriage and caused each other some deep wounds that took a long time to overcome.

In our opinion, a friendship that brings down your marriage is not a friendship worth having. In the end, your marriage matters the most. If one spouse has a relationship that is harming the marriage, then that relationship probably needs to go.

Ultimately, we encourage you to find couples you both enjoy. This is the best ongoing approach for your relationship. It may require reaching outside your comfort zone, inviting people into your home and investing in new friend-

Kelly and Tosha Williams

ships. Though it will take time for meaningful relationships to grow, these will surely bless your marriage.

Discuss the relational burdens you bear for each other. Talk about the friends you have and friends you wish you could have. Talk about whether you need a new relational strategy in your marriage. Be willing to bear the relational burdens your spouse needs you to bear for the sake of your marriage.

Children Burdens

Children are the litmus test for the selfish factor in your marriage. Ultimately, we think this is positive because, through our children, we have to make choices to be selfless. Selfless choices make us better parents *and* better spouses.

Children can make you look at your spouse and fall in love with him all over again because you recognize the sacrifice involved. On the other hand, children may cause you to look at your spouse with disdain because of her lack of appreciation for the sacrifices you make on behalf of the family.

This one does not work itself out overnight. Some couples go through the challenges of making their own babies; other couples go through the rigors of adopting their babies; other marriages start with instant families from previous marriages or relationships. Once you have children, you have them around for a long, long time. They change and complicate your life in every way.

However, children do not make marriage hard. Marriage is hard in and of itself; children only make it harder. Ask your spouse the question, "What burdens do you carry on my behalf because of the children?" This could be a long conversation.

As you share these burdens, do not be resentful. Talk about the burdens you bear for your children with joy. Share them as trophies of accomplishments. Wear them as scars that show the battle marks of sacrifices. In our opinion, there is no greater sacrifice than to sacrifice for your spouse because of your children. Why? Because this leaves a legacy in your children that they will carry into the next generation. This shows them a living example of what it looks like to be selfless in a world saturated with selfishness.

After your long discussion, ask, "What burdens do you need me to carry for you because of the kids?" This may be the most practical question of all. You may hear some answers like these: pick up the kids after school twice a week; give me a regular night out by myself so I can recover from the exhaustion; cook dinner once a week so I don't have to be in the kitchen all the time; don't make me always have to be the disciplinarian. Ask the question, and let your spouse fill in the blanks.

In-Law Burdens

When a couple marries, they must leave their parents and become one with each other. We have met very few couples for whom this transition has been altogether easy.

Most couples carry burdens in this area, us included. For some, this burden is a marriage killer. Gratefully, we can say that our own in-law burdens have lessened with time, and hopefully yours will as well. Time has a way of giving you, the younger generation, a chance to grow up and not be threatened by the powers that be. Time also has a way of giving the older generation a perspective about your marriage that they did not have in the early days of your marriage.

There are exceptions to this rule, of course. Time may not heal this wound for your marriage. You may always carry some heavy burdens for your spouse regarding in-laws. Your spouse may have to continually struggle underneath the weight of this burden for your family. *It is important, though, that neither of you shove the other away for the sake of your parents.* While you may grapple with in-law issues for the rest of your life, we have a few suggestions to guide you.

If there is an in-law conflict in your marriage, you should each deal with your own family. Your parents, siblings or relatives will probably always love you to some degree, but they may not always love your spouse.

If your parents make you choose between your spouse and them, always choose your spouse. Fight for your spouse and demand respect for that person. If your parents want a relationship with you, they need to understand that from your perspective this is a package deal: you and your spouse are the package. If your parents will not accept that, then choose your spouse.

On the other hand, your spouse is something of a package deal with his family. If you do not like your in-laws, do not punish your spouse because of it. It is not his fault; he did not get to choose his parents. If you have a hard time with your in-laws, do not give your spouse an ultimatum. The burden you may bear for your spouse is to work out some type of agreement where there can be as much harmony as possible in the relationship. This is a huge challenge, but it will speak volumes when you sacrifice for the sake of your spouse.

In addition, refuse to make your in-law struggles your kids' struggles. Your children have a right to have a relationship with their grandparents. Unless there is blatant abuse from which you need to protect them, you are only hurting your kids (most of the time) if you do not help foster this relationship.

Sit down with your spouse and ask what burdens she bears for you because of your family. Listen to what your spouse has to say. Sympathize with these feelings. It will be an incredible temptation to be defensive. You must force yourself to be quiet and listen, or you may find your marriage shipwrecked by this burden. You have to carry this burden together.

After the dust settles, then ask the question, "What burdens do you need me to carry for you because of my parents?" Half the battle is listening. If your spouse feels heard—truly heard—you might be amazed at how much lower his expectations are of you once he knows he is not alone in this battle.

Ready for the Good Stuff

As the two of us talk through the burdens described in this chapter, we become more aware of how we help, protect and strengthen one another. Sometimes in the craziness of life, we tend to merely survive and do what it takes to get by. However, slowing down and recognizing how we make a huge difference in each other's lives makes us appreciate the relationship we share. By supporting each other, we help our "Fantasy Meet Reality" because, for us, grateful hearts become more giving hearts.

You may feel overwhelmed by the discussion of burdens in this chapter and by the challenge to "take up your cross."

We understand that, but we encourage you not to give up. As you and your spouse bear burdens and "take up your cross" for each other, you will find that the burdens become lighter and the cross becomes easier to carry. The two of you are working with each other, on behalf of each other. This should fill your hearts with gratitude, which can be an incredible impetus to fantasy. You engage your spouse in new ways of fantasy because you are so thankful for how that person engages you in reality. This is what REAL marriage looks like.

Relationships are complicated and sometimes they are hard, but few things are more rewarding than REAL marriage with your spouse. The sacrifice is worth it. We want to encourage you to take up these burdens.

Up to this point in the book, you have learned to *Realize the Cost*. You understand the price of your relationship, and you have determined to pay it. You have also read about how to *Embrace Spiritual Guideposts*. You even persisted in figuring out how to *Align Your Will* to your spouse.

Through these, you have learned the first three parts of REAL. You have done what it takes to stay on the ship, bail water and strengthen the hull of your relationship. You are practicing the dance of a great marriage. You are working on learning how to battle offensively for your marriage. You are bearing burdens for each other.

Now it is time for the good stuff. In the next section, we will look at the last part of REAL: *Love Each Other*. The fun is about to begin.

Why don't you let it start tonight? Slide your toe under the covers and touch your spouse's toe as a reminder that you still have a connection. The two of you have toes that link your feet together, and you are creating a "thousand strands" that bind your hearts together.

Most definitely, you are carefully writing your own personal "story of us," and your chapters are getting more compelling every day!

Discussion Questions:

1. Of the burdens described, which do you carry for your spouse?

2. Which burden do you struggle with the most to carry for your spouse?

3. Which burden do you feel your spouse least realizes you carry for her? This may be the same as the difficult burden in question two, or it may be entirely different. Tell your spouse about this, then find out what burden she carries for you that you did not realize.

4. Which burden do you least know how to carry for your spouse? Where can you find help or guidance for this?

5. What burden do you most wish your spouse would help you carry? In a loving way, communicate this to your partner.

6. How have you expressed your gratitude to your spouse for the burdens he carries for you? How could you show more appreciation to him?

7. The burdens are part of the reality of your marriage. Are you ready for some fantasy? We are going to talk more about that in this last section. Until then, how might you have some fun tonight?

　　　　　　　Kelly and Tosha Williams

Section Four:

Love Each Other

13. the leading

*"I never thought this was going to happen to me and Ben.
I thought we were going to be the ones to go the distance.
But I just couldn't seem to get him to put down the
purple crayon."*
("That's Ben ... he's the one you fell in love with.")
- Katie and her friend talking, in The Story of Us

For our wedding ceremony, the two of us wrote our own vows. We each put a great deal of thought into these as we envisioned what promises to make at the wedding altar. Whether they came out as feeble or eloquent, these words were our attempt to set the stage for "happily ever after."

On our big day, we repeated the traditional vows after the minister. Then we each spoke our own personalized promises of love. As Tosha looked at me through teary eyes, I said my vows first:

I, Kelly, take you, Tosha, to be my wife.

With God's help, I promise to exhibit the Spirit's fruits in our marriage.

I promise to be peaceful and patient.

I promise to show you kindness, gentleness and self-control.

I promise to remain faithful to our vows and to the call God has given me.

And, Tosha, I promise you my love,

that asks only to lead you,

to provide for you and protect you,

and to cherish you as long as we both shall live.

After Kelly finished declaring his promises, I spoke next. Emotion overwhelmed me as I pledged these sacred words:

I, Tosha, take you, Kelly, to be my husband.

And I promise to be your faithful wife,

to honor and to respect you,

to obey you as Christ commands,

to forgive you and to ask forgiveness, to be your encouragement,

to commit myself to your happiness and well-being,

and to share every part of life with you as long as we both shall live.

This is my solemn vow before our God and our loved ones.

After we spoke these vows on that sunny day back in 1993,

we embarked on the adventure of marriage with high hopes and big dreams.

Promises, Promises

We made promises on our wedding day and, if you are married, so did you. In fact, every married couple reading this book made the same promise on their wedding day: to love each other for a lifetime. The words and expressions of this promise may have been different for everybody, but the intent was the same: *I will love you for the rest of my life.* We all embark in marriage with the highest of expectations.

Somewhere between the altar and the third child, mortgage or business venture, though, life gets in the way of love. The commitment of love may still be there—which is a good thing—but the passion of love may be far removed from daily life. The two of us have experienced this in our marriage, and we have talked with enough people to know that most couples have.

One thing is for sure: you do not stay where you are in love. Love cannot be stagnant. The stuff of your life takes you somewhere. Will your passion for your spouse go with it? How *do* you love your spouse for the rest of your life?

The "You" I Promised To

Do you know *who* you fell in love with? Of course you know this person's name—but do you really know your spouse? What uniqueness initially drew you to your wife? What was it that set your husband apart from all the other guys you dated? What was it about your wife made her "the one"?

Katie described what attracted her to Ben, saying,

> "When I was in college, we had to write a term paper…on any book we considered to be the one that best depicted how we viewed the world…
>
> "I did my paper on *Harold and the Purple Crayon*. It's a small book about a little boy who draws the world the way he wants it to be with his magic crayon…
>
> "I just loved that book because it was about everything that I wasn't…"

Katie married Ben because he had all the traits she loved but did not have. Certainly, to some extent, this was true of you, too, when you fell in love with your spouse and got married.

The question is, do these intricacies of your spouse still enamor you? Does his random sense of humor still mesmerize you? Does her coy demeanor still fascinate you? Or do you now struggle to love the traits that once drew you to love your spouse?

As a pastor, I have performed many wedding ceremonies. I have been at weddings where the bride was so jittery that she could not see straight. I have officiated weddings where the groom was so anxious he could hardly breathe. Oh, the stories I could tell! When it comes to weddings, I have seen many different things.

Yet, in all the weddings I have attended or officiated, I have never been at a wedding where the "you" in the wedding vows was followed by a list of qualifications. I have never heard a vow ceremony where the groom said, "I will love you for the rest of my life…if you don't get fat after having a baby, if you cook gourmet cuisine every night and if you have sex six times a week with me." I have never heard a bride say, "I will love you for the rest of my life … if you don't go bald and get a gut, if you immediately complete the honey-do list and if you let us spend every holiday with my family."

Prenuptials and nagging doubts aside, odds are that nobody pulls out a list of qualifications to recite at their wedding ceremony. This just does not happen. When you promise to love, you vow to love a person: *I* promise to love *you*. End of sentence. When you say your vows, you do not list exceptions to the rule or qualifications that must be met.

Instead, you make a blanket statement. On your wedding day, you looked your future spouse in the eye and said, in words and in actions, "I am linking who I am to who you are."

Loving "You"

"You" is an easy person to love when you like everything about that person, even the way he colors outside the lines with purple crayon. "You" is a great person to make promises to when your eyes are star struck with fantasy and dreams. "You" is a wonderful person to marry when life is covered with wedding veils, beautiful flowers and confetti.

"You" is not so breathtaking, though, when his marks outside the lines become messes you have to clean up. "You" may not be so enticing when she begins to prefer her flannel nightgown and bunny slippers to her sexy honeymoon teddy. "You" may get a little harder to keep promises to when he will not find a job. "You" becomes more difficult to handle when her personality traits become more irritating than interesting.

Yet, that "you" is the person *you* made your wedding vows to. *I will love you for the rest of my life.* How do you love your spouse for who he is, not for who you wish he were?

Before we answer this all-important question, we need to recap what we have experienced together through the first twelve chapters.

Each one of us has had to *Realize the Cost* and pay a great price for REAL marriage. You realize that cost daily, some days more than other days. You have decided that you are not going to live in "Fantasy Versus Reality," nor are you going to accept "Fantasy Drowned by Reality." You have determined to *Realize the Cost* so that your "Fantasy Meets Reality." You are going to do what it takes to make your marriage special, no matter what life throws your way.

As you *Realize the Cost*, you have then accepted the call to *Embrace Spiritual Guideposts* for your REAL marriage. You understand that, by following the Ancient Guideposts established by the Creator of life and marriage, your marriage has its best chance to be successful.

Living by the guideposts and paying the price for your marriage have forced you to deal with the struggles your marriage faces. This has required you to *Align Your Will* to one another by being selfless and battling for each other. You take up the daily burdens that your spouse needs you to carry in marriage. You are intentional about submitting to and sacrificing for your spouse.

In all of this, you have begun the dance of vulnerability and created an environment for REAL marriage. We are thrilled you have come this far.

Now it is time to *Love Each Other* in REAL marriage.

Kelly and Tosha Williams

In this last section of the book, we have one more acronym for you. We will take the word "love" and use each letter to describe to you *how* to love your spouse in a REAL marriage. Here is what "LOVE" stands for:

"**L**eading"–you lead by demonstrating the characteristics of love

"**O**ffering"–you offer yourself to your spouse

"**V**aluing"–you value new experiences for your marriage

"**E**mbracing"–you embrace the greatest love story ever

We believe that REAL love begins with "Leading in Love." We can find a path for how to do this by looking into the Ancient Scriptures, which say:

> God is love...As we live in God, our love grows more perfect...Such love has no fear, because perfect love expels all fear...We love each other because He loved us first.
>
> from 1 John 4:16–19

God took the initiative in love when He loved us *first*; this is what leadership is. As we learn about love from God, then we can follow His example. We love well when we "Lead in Love" in marriage.

"I fell in love with her at first sight," is an endearing example of being the first to love. "The first time I met him, I knew he was the man I'd marry," is another romantic way someone might describe an initial encounter with love. Leading in love takes this initiative to love your spouse far beyond the beginning of your relationship. It extends into every aspect, day and year of your marriage. When you "Lead in Love," you pour the characteristics of love on your spouse from the day you marry until the day one of you dies.

The Leading

How each of us live out our vows is how we lead in our marriage relationship. The way that I love Kelly is to love the "you" that he was, is and will become. When we got married, I said, "I promise ... to share every part of life with you." With those words, I promised to love the entirety of Kelly, who he is, not just who he was or who I wish he would be. The way that I lead in our marriage now is to live out my vows, when Kelly is in a good mood and when he is in a bad mood. He experiences the fulfillment of my vows when I love him no matter if he is dressed up, handsome and powerful, or if he is grubby, sick and annoying.

Kelly may change. In fact, he already has and will some more. However, the promises I made to him do not. The same is true for you. Your spouse will change; your promises do not. This is how you "Lead in Love."

For REAL marriage, the Ancient Scriptures describe leadership in the following passage. Interestingly, this passage follows verses that distinctly dwell on marriage, so we have paraphrased this passage to make it specific to marriage, too. When life is short but the days are long, the following words exemplify how you "Lead in Love" in your marriage:

> Each of you married couples, be of one mind, full of sympathy toward each other, loving one another with tender hearts and humble minds. Don't repay evil for evil.

Don't retaliate when your spouse says unkind things to you or about you. Instead, pay your spouse back with a blessing. That is what God wants you to do, and He will bless you for it. If you want a happy marriage and good days, keep your tongue from speaking evil and keep your lips from telling lies.

Turn away from evil and do good. Work hard at living in peace with your spouse. The eyes of the Lord watch over those who do right and His ears are open to their prayers. But the Lord turns His face against those who do evil to their spouse.

1 Peter 3:8–12 paraphrase

You "Lead in Love" by demonstrating the character required for REAL marriage. We have talked about what this looks like throughout the book, but we want to extrapolate some specific principles from this passage.

"Leadership in Love" is not a dictatorship by either partner; rather, it is mutual submission. Leadership in marriage is neither the husband always getting the final say nor the wife always being in control. With mutual submission, REAL marriage works out beautifully, because the two of you each lead by putting the other before yourself. When you are "of one mind," you are writing your personal "story of us" as a team, and you are filling its pages with the intertwined chapters of your lives.

Leadership in marriage is not repaying evil for evil but—each of you—seeking to show good to the other. Leadership in marriage is not retaliating but forgiving. This is easier said than done, especially when your spouse is careless about your feelings or hard-hearted about your desires. You may encounter huge obstacles in this area. Nonetheless, leadership sometimes involves turning your face to the wind and walking into it with determination. When you say, *I will love you even through this,* you are a leader of the most noble sort.

Leadership in marriage is not insulting your spouse's weaknesses and exposing these to others. Rationalizations such as "if he were more like me" or "if she would think through this like I do" are not ways to lead. You are who you are; your spouse is who he is. Do not look at all your spouse's weaknesses and compare those to your strengths. Do not judge all the areas your spouse is *supposed* to be strong in, like male and female stereotypes. Your wife may not be a good cook, but she surely has other areas where she excels. Your husband may not be able to fix a leaky faucet, but he certainly has other positive traits about him. Lead your spouse by validating what she is good at instead of belittling what she cannot do well. Identify the positive in your spouse and praise it!

When you lead in marriage, you choose to compensate for your spouse's weaknesses with your own strengths. We are not implying that you should carry the entire load of the household if your spouse is irresponsible. There are situations where you must draw a line and create firm boundaries for yourself.

In a normal marriage that seeks to be REAL, though, you lead by *complimenting* your spouse's strengths and *complementing* your spouse's weaknesses. Do you see the distinction here? Leadership in a REAL marriage means you bring your best strengths into marriage and submit these to your spouse in order to help your spouse in the areas where he is weak. And vice versa. Instead of letting your spouse's weaknesses irritate you, look for how your strengths can *complement* his weak-

Kelly and Tosha Williams

nesses and make him a better person. Instead of feeling inferior to your wife because of what she does well, *compliment* her strengths and tell her how she makes you a better person. This is a significant way that you can bless your spouse.

When you "Lead in Love," you give your spouse the benefit of the doubt instead of assuming the worst. This is how you battle *for* each other instead of *against* each other. Giving one another the benefit of the doubt demonstrates sympathy, tenderness and consideration.

It is often easier to try to control your spouse than to give him the benefit of the doubt. You must choose to exchange your control for trust. You must make a decision that you will trust your spouse, even if he processes things differently than you do, even if she does things differently than you.

There may come a time when you give your spouse the benefit of the doubt but she blows it. Your spouse may fail you; your spouse may have to make a confession to you. Believe it or not, even this can give your marriage a chance to grow—if you will let it. You will have the opportunity to stand in the gap for your marriage and use your strengths to rebuild your hurting partner. This is how you can bless your spouse, and this may come full circle to build more trust in your relationship. Someday you are going to need your spouse to do the same for you when *you* mess up, too.

If you "Lead in Love," you will do *good* for your spouse. One year, Kelly proclaimed it "the year of Tosha" in our marriage. Throughout the year, he did nice things for me, like taking me on a few special shopping trips and giving me some unique surprises. By the end of the year, I felt so loved, appreciated and blessed. Kelly figured out what made me happy, and you can be assured that I made *him* happy as a result! Surprise your spouse with kindness. *You* may be surprised at how the good comes back around!

To "Lead in Love," you put a *lot* of effort into creating peace in your relationship. This peace is not the let's-just-do-whatever-it-takes-to-be-happy-and-quit-arguing sort of false peace that the Surrenderer employs when facing conflict in a selfish mode. The peace mentioned in this Scripture is the true kind, where the two of you honestly communicate, are fully known and are completely accepted. *This* is REAL marriage of the best sort!

As you demonstrate the character required to "Lead in Love," the Ancient Scriptures say that you will be blessed and your marriage will be blessed, too. This may not be easy, but it is so worthwhile.

A Word on Structure

Now, when we refer to leadership in marriage, you might be thinking, "Here we go again. Here is another book on how the woman is to submit and the man is to rule in order to have a good marriage." No, that is not our point.

Neither in our own marriage nor in this book are we focused primarily on the leadership *structure* in marriage. We are most concerned with the *content* and *character* of leadership in the relationship. We believe that *who you are* is more important than *who you are in charge of.*

Granted, not everybody sees leadership in marriage this way. Some people focus primarily on the leadership structure of the marriage relationship. They sincerely believe that the outward structure of a marriage relationship determines its health. In their opinion, the husband is the ultimate authority and the wife must always submit to him in order for a couple to have a good marriage. This is a simplistic description of the "hierarchical" view.

Other couples prefer to function in what is called an "egalitarian" marriage, where both husband and wife have equal say. Still other marriages work out different means of structure.

From our perspective, debating which leadership structure is best and who is supposed to be in charge of a marriage does not really matter at this point. You can argue about that all the way to the divorce courts. We want to focus not on *who* is in charge when we discuss leadership, but on *what it looks like* to demonstrate loving leadership to each other in marriage.

Do we believe there is a structure to marriage? Yes, but rarely is it necessary to go there. We believe that the husband is responsible to be the lead servant of the marriage and that while ultimately both partners should submit, the wife is held further accountable for it. That said, though, submission is not something that Kelly can demand, and lead servanthood is not something Tosha can demand. These are gifts that we choose to give to one another because of the character and content of our REAL marriage.

In today's fragmented society, many in our generation come from broken homes and marriages. "Submission" and "structure" are dirty words because people have never seen these lived in healthy, positive ways. Even though you may have never seen submission and structure lived well in marriage, these are wonderful aspects of REAL marriage. Nonetheless, because these terms have so much negative baggage, we believe that "Leading in Love" is such an important concept.

Without the content and character of REAL marriage, the debate over who is in charge is a moot point. No one, male or female, is going to care about these structural issues apart from the content and characteristics of REAL love being present. When you both "Lead in Love" in your marriage, then the proper structure for your marriage will more easily fall into place.

Rediscovering "You"

In the movie *The Story of Us*, Katie and Ben just cannot reconcile their differences, so they decide to divorce. When Katie admits this to her friend, she describes how Ben always does things his own way. He always colors outside the lines with his own purple crayon. Katie used to find that attractive. Now, Ben's traits that she had fallen in love with are driving her crazy. The idea of *Harold and the Magic Crayon* is not so mesmerizing anymore. Instead of enjoying Ben's uniqueness, Katie is fully irritated with the caveats of his personality, saying:

> "The problem in a marriage is, if one person is always Harold–drawing the world the way they want it to be–the other person has no choice but to draw it the way it is. Which is probably why they never wrote a book about Harold's wife."

Ben's marks outside the lines bother her, and so does his purple crayon. She cannot take it anymore. Katie's friend will not accept that as an excuse, though. After hearing Katie vent her frustration, her friend wisely responds,

"That's Ben ... he's the one you fell in love with."

That is the point in *The Story of Us*. It is also a huge point in your personal "story of us." Your husband will change in some ways that you do not want him to change. Your wife will not change in areas where you desperately want her to change. Your wedding vows did not come with qualifications, though. You said, in so many words on your wedding day, *I will love you for the rest of my life.*

Somehow, Katie's friend makes an impact on her thought process. Toward the end of the movie, Katie implores Ben:

"Let's face it, anybody's going to have traits that get on your nerves. I mean, why shouldn't it be *your* annoying traits, and I'm no day at the beach (but I do have a good sense of direction so at least I can find the beach, which is not a criticism of yours, it's just a strength of mine). And ... you're a good friend and good friends are hard to find."

There *are* no perfect friends in life, just as there is no perfect spouse. As Katie finally realizes this truth about life and relationship, this revelation helps her "Lead in Love" and pursue Ben's heart. Although Ben is not a perfect man, he is a good man—and he is an intricate part of Katie's story.

Instead of trying "to take the purple crayon" out of your spouse's hand, start rediscovering why you chose this person in the first place. You chose your spouse because this person brought things to your story that you wanted or admired. Don't forget this when you get into the throes of your relationship.

The person who chooses to "Lead in Love" chooses to let go of the control and the criticism. Instead, you embrace your spouse's nuances and look for ways to help your partner's uniqueness blossom in marriage. In REAL marriage, you lead by using your influence to help your spouse excel.

You did not marry just anybody; you married someone who understood your hopes and dreams, who was passionate with you, who "got" you. You married the person who was the love of your life. Resist letting time or work, pain or struggles steal these pages of your story.

Instead, accept your husband for who he is, purple crayons, rough edges, farts and all. Embrace your wife for who she is, long showers, lost keys, PMS and everything else.

You need not be a threat to one another. You are a compliment, a complement, a completion to one another. On your wedding day, you promised to love each other. So, love well! This is your life; this is your "story of us." Do not settle for pages and pages of anger, resentment, distrust or retaliation in your marriage. Fill your chapters with unity and tenderness, blessing and peace. This is how you "Lead in Love."

In the midst of your reality, you live out the fantasy you began on your wedding day: *I will love you for the rest of my life.*

The rhythm becomes stronger every day; you begin moving to the music together. The dance of fantasy and reality is about to get more enticing than ever.

Kelly and Tosha Williams

For Discussion:

1. Describe to your husband the things he brings to your life that you could not live without. Tell your wife about what made you fall in love with her in the first place. Take time to remember and talk about your spouse's traits that enamored you in the beginning.

2. What "purple crayons" does your spouse use that drives you crazy? Were these propensities in your spouse when you married, and if so, how did you feel about them back then?

3. How do you give your spouse the benefit of the doubt? In what ways do you tend to assume the worst?

4. In what ways are you negative toward your spouse? When do you speak negatively about your spouse in front of other people? If you are joking, does your spouse take it as a joke? (Let your spouse answer this!) Do you need to ask forgiveness in this area of your relationship?

5. Are there strengths you have that your marriage is not utilizing? Are there weaknesses your spouse has that you can better complement? Discuss these and how you can make your marriage better.

6. How can you let your spouse shine in the areas where he is really capable, strong or talented?

7. In marriage, 1+1=1. This does not make logical math sense, but the longer you are married the more you realize that the two of you begin to merge into one. How can you mutually submit in new ways to one another so that your combined strengths and weaknesses make for a very strong "one"?

8. What are some ways that you can bless your spouse and do

good to that person this week? Start thinking about a long-term plan for how you can bless your partner.

9. What are some unique elements in your personal "story of us"?

Kelly and Tosha Williams

14. the offering

> *"I would rather have sex with my husband any day than kiss him. Kissing seems so intimate."*
> *- friend's comment in* The Story of Us

The evening had a cool wind that made the trees sway. The moon was bright and made the rocks and hills glow. It was a perfect night for passion, and we took advantage of the opportunity. A deserted park, an empty parking lot and, well, you can imagine the rest.

What you may not be able to (or want to!) imagine is that we were not young lovers having sex by moonlight. We had been married for over twelve years. We laughed at ourselves because here we were, many years into our relationship, still hot for each other. It was our sixteenth dating anniversary; our goal for the evening was to start working on this book. We had already been out to a nice dinner and were headed to a coffee shop to begin brainstorming. Somewhere along the way, though, Kelly took the scenic route, and then we made a little detour to passion.

Sure, we had to move a couple of car seats and throw some toys out of the way. Other than that, though, we were feeling alive and sexual and very much in love. The world was ours, and we enjoyed the fantasy together. Sex, we decided, was the perfect way to initiate the start of this book.

Still laughing, we crawled back in the front seats and continued on our way to the coffee shop. Once there, we settled into the more serious undertaking of figuring out some ideas and principles for this book. As our computer filled with our thoughts and words, however, we could not help but overhear and observe other people. It was obvious that there were many other people experiencing sex that night, too.

We watched a couple come in out of the cold weather. The girl was wearing a spaghetti strap dress, which in the middle of a Colorado winter is not a good idea unless you are hot as a stolen pistol. The guy headed straight to the restroom and came out wearing a different pair of pants. Hmm.... As they waited for their coffees and stroked one another, it was not too difficult to figure out what was on their agenda that night.

Behind us, we overheard two teenage girls and a teenage boy exchange sexual innuendoes as they sipped their lattes. Soon the innuendos became an open discussion about sex. When the three left abruptly, it was not hard to imagine their plans.

Like it or not, most everybody has sex. We do, you do, married couples do and unmarried couples do. Teenagers have sex. Gays, bisexuals and straights have sex. Just about everybody has sex. That night put quite the perspective on it for us. Sex may be the most overrated activity in the world, but it is still the best one out there.

The Big Difference

Everywhere we look and listen, be it in a coffee shop, at school or in the office, we see sexuality in our culture. From the television to the radio to the bookstore, sex is all over. You can watch it, you can talk it, you can read it and you can do it. Whether it is brief or enduring, sexuality makes us feel alive. We all want to *feel* something, we all want to be loved and we all, at some point, want to have sex.

So, if sex is an element of most every romantic relationship, then what sets it apart for REAL marriage? If everybody has sex, then what makes it different for your marriage? Is sex just sex, or is there more to it? If there is more, then what is it?

We believe that what sets sex apart in REAL marriage is the offering, not the taking. We as a married couple can sit at one table in a coffee shop, talk about sex and get excited; three teenagers can sit at a table next to us, talk about sex and get excited; a couple can make a pit stop to change soaked pants, talk about more sex and get excited. We can all experience sexuality the same night.

In time, however, the reality of relationships are revealed, not through the sex, but through the love. Five years from now, who from that coffee shop filled with sex talk will still be having great sex? The ones who had REAL love. Sex alone cannot keep a relationship together. Offering yourself in love can. This is an enormous difference.

Offering Yourself

Sex outside REAL relationship (and by that we do not just mean sex outside marriage) is about taking instead of giving. It is like buying on credit. You can enjoy your purchases for a while; in fact, you can *really* enjoy them.

Eventually, though, you will max out your line of credit and the credit bill will come due. Whether you want to or not, you will have to start making payments or go down into the abyss of emotional bankruptcy. This goes for every sexual relationship outside a REAL marriage.

In the bank of your marriage, though, you can store up the means to pay for great sex. The first three letters of REAL—which we have discussed throughout this book—is what will make those payments. When you *Realize the Cost* of a great relationship and choose to pay that price, when you *Embrace Spiritual Guideposts* in your relationship and keep your commitment to follow them, when you *Align Your Will* to your spouse and battle for that person, *then* you are able to really *Love Each Other*.

We believe the love in REAL marriage shows up in the passion you feel and sex you experience. In the last chapter, we talked about the "L" of love—"Lead in Love." Now we want to look at the "O" of love—"**O**ffer Yourself." Whereas a solely sexual relationship is primarily about fulfilling one's own sexual desires and fantasies, sex in REAL relationship is about discovering the fantasy of your partner and "**O**ffering Yourself" to fulfill that fantasy. It is not about meeting your own needs; it is about each of you meeting your spouse's needs.

Long after the teenagers have left the coffee shop, had their sex and lost their selfish passion, your REAL marriage is just getting started with experiencing sexual fulfillment. Your great sex is only beginning, because true passion flourishes over time in an environment of selflessness.

As you well know, though, selflessness does not simply happen in marriage. It requires leadership and intentionality. As we discussed in the last chapter, "Leading in Love" is selflessly fulfilling your vows to your spouse. In this chapter, "Offering Yourself" is being intentional to fulfill your spouse's needs and desires.

This, really, is the highest form of love. It is saying to your spouse, *I will love you for the rest of my life, and I will give myself for you.*

Putting your spouse's needs before your own is when sex becomes more than sex. This sets the mood for the best of passionate fantasy.

The Passion Behind Sex

Are you still "Offering Yourself" in marriage? Your mind may be going through a whole list of ways you feel you offer yourself to your spouse ... doing the laundry, bringing home the bacon, putting up with bad habits, cooking meals, caring for the kids. Certainly, "Offering Yourself" in these ways creates an environment of selflessness and confidence in which your sex life can grow and flourish. These do not guarantee you feel loved by each other sexually, however. Sex is most often required to accomplish that.

How are you "Offering Yourself" sexually to your spouse? Are you willing to go parking if that is what your husband wants? Are you willing to give an all-over massage if that is what heats up your wife? Are you willing to try a new position, play a new game, model a new outfit for the sake of "**O**ffering Yourself" to your spouse?

If you are not willing, if you have stopped offering yourselves to each other sexually, then you have begun the slow death of becoming a marriage that is about the transference of information. This is when you get to the place in your marriage that you share information but no longer the passion you once had. For example, "I paid the bills ... I'll pick up the kids after work ... I'll grab that at the store ... The repairman is coming next Wednesday."

Yes, every marriage has transference of information. You cannot survive without it because you have to communicate information with each other. However, when that is all your marriage is, then, in essence, it is more of a business partnership or roommate arrangement than a passionate REAL marriage.

Marriage was never intended to be primarily about the transference of information. What makes marriage unique is the transference of passion. Passion involves every element of who you are, starting with your physical body but certainly not ending there. We are made for passion. We are made for something more than grocery lists, nine-to-five jobs and dirty diapers. The essence of our beings long for passion. Our souls yearn to come alive.

On your wedding day, you promised to pursue this with your spouse. Time and pain may have come between you, making passion a thing of the past. But your marriage is designed for more. Marriage is about sharing your entire life, not only the easy or convenient parts. Your bodies belong to each other, not to abuse, but to enjoy.

In our marriage, we do not just want to know the necessary things about life from each other; we want each other. We want to be with each other and experience each other. Of course, there are ebbs and flows to passion. We cannot be hot for each other every single minute of every day for a lifetime. We have already established the fact that we cannot forever live in the honeymoon stage of "Fantasy Apart from Reality."

We can delight in each other along life's way, however. On a regular, consistent basis, REAL marriage must transfer not only information but also passion. This is how "Fantasy Meets Reality."

Fulfilling Your Spouse's Fantasy

When you are spouse-centered rather than self-centered, you help your spouse experience his fantasy. Fantasy is what your spouse desires for pleasure. Once you have determined to live by the guideposts established in Ancient Scriptures, you are the one—the only one—who can give your spouse this satisfaction in the sexual realm. Sometimes I look at Tosha and say, "If I don't get it from you, I won't be getting it. So will you give it to me ... tonight?"

At the crossroads in our marriage, we choose to live as one, to enjoy sex, to keep having sex and to seek fulfillment together. We have determined to keep sex sacred in our relationship, according to the guideposts established in Ancient Scriptures. These are our guiding principles in fantasy. With these in mind, it is our inside joke that if Kelly is ever going to see a naked model, it has to be Tosha. If Tosha is ever going to experience orgasm, it has to be with Kelly.

That is probably more than you want to know, and it is certainly on the border of more than we want to say! Nonetheless, this principle of REAL marriage is true: you are the only one who can and should fulfill your spouse's fantasy in the sexual realm. This is how you "**O**ffer Yourself" in love.

What does your spouse long for in life, in your sexual relationship? What did she wish for when you first got married? What did he love to do when your sexual relationship was new? What is your partner's passionate fantasy? What arouses your wife? What words do you use to provoke fantasy in the reality of your sexual relationship? What does your husband enjoy physically, sexually? Do you know?

You talked with your spouse about fantasy way back at the beginning of this book. Take a risk and talk about it again, on an even deeper level. Because you have developed new vulnerability along the way, you may be surprised at what you hear. Once you know what your spouse's fantasy is, take a risk and "**O**ffer Yourself" to fulfill that.

More Than Sex

Sex, for most relationships, is a means for people to fulfill their own fantasies. In REAL marriage, sex becomes a passionate expression of gratitude and connectedness. This is unique to marriage and marriage alone. Moving beyond yourself in order to fulfill your spouse's fantasies is what progresses your marriage to "Fantasy Meets Reality."

Just as you are made for more than sex, though, life is about more than sex. Your spouse certainly has many wishes and dreams, hopes and fantasies in areas besides sex. You can offer yourself to fulfill your spouse's fantasy in seven common areas of relationship:

- Physical
- Verbal
- Emotional
- Spiritual
- Relational
- Cognitive
- Sexual

The more you offer of yourself to your spouse, the more you will live out love and the more your spouse will feel loved. When Kelly offers himself to me in the way that I need him, I feel loved. Sometimes this is in conversation, when I really want us to talk. Sometimes I want him to offer himself to me in the spiritual realm, so I can connect with another human about what the Creator is speaking into my life. Sometimes I simply need Kelly to try to understand me when my emotions are going haywire. These are all ways he can offer himself to me outside our sexual relationship.

Sometimes I offer myself to Kelly by putting the kids to bed by myself when he has had a rough day. There are other times when I, the "stay-at-home" wife, take a shower and fix my hair before Kelly comes home so that he has an attractive wife to greet him. These are ways that I can offer myself to him. Unlike some other burdens and offerings, these are not hard, but they can have a huge effect on our marriage.

Sometimes we struggle as a couple and do not even know what to offer each other. In times like these, it is sometimes helpful to watch a movie that provokes emotion and use that as our starting point for discussion.

Of course, *The Story of Us* has a scene about this that provokes a conversation for us. As Katie is at lunch with two friends, this dialogue occurs:

> "Larry really wanted to have sex last night; he even gave me the thirty-second massage..." one friend confides.
>
> "So, did you make love?" Katie queries.
>
> "Well, I couldn't, I was just too tired!"
>
> "How did you get out of it?" their other friend asks.
>
> "Well, I pretended to fall asleep during the massage; I even did that heavy breathing thing... But the whole thing backfired, because when I really fell asleep the baby started crying, and then Larry pretended that he was asleep..."
>
> "Fool!" her friend interrupts her. "If he had just gotten up with the baby, you would have sounded the trumpets, opened the gates and welcomed the troops home for Christmas!"
>
> "In a heartbeat," the weary friend agrees.

While this conversation is a little frank, it is a great example of the truth about "**O**ffering Yourself." Giving more than the obligatory thirty-second massage, caring for the baby and having sex are all parts of giving yourself to one another. These are all pieces of a whole that create a deep connection for your marriage.

"**O**ffering Yourself" produces an intimacy that sex alone cannot. This is powerful because it creates deposits in the bank of your marriage. When you offer all that you are, you are creating an environment for passion to be expressed and fantasy to be fulfilled. Don't you want to experience that?

We sure do, which is why we took a risk that night of our sixteenth dating anniversary. It is why we still try to engage, no matter how stressful or busy life is. It is why we continually seek to live out REAL marriage. "Offering Yourself" to your spouse is not always easy, but it is so worth it.

In the next chapter, we are going to talk more specifically about ways to take your fantasy to a deeper level through "Valuing New Experiences." You are doing the hard work of REAL, and now your marriage is going to keep getting more interesting!

For Discussion:

1. If the term "fantasy" has a negative connotation for you, spend some time unpacking why that is. Then, if necessary, substitute a different term for "fantasy," such as "dream," "wish" or "desire." Talk about this for your marriage. What would you each love to experience?

2. In what ways do you long for your spouse? By this, we are asking about sexual offerings as well as other offerings.

3. How are you offering yourself sexually to your spouse?

4. Have you quit offering any of these areas to your spouse? If so, which ones and how?

5. Are there parts you have never offered? Why? Talk about why you don't offer them. Do you have valid reasons? Does your spouse consider these valid?

6. What do you desire your spouse to offer to you? Talk about this.

7. When did you last go parking? What are you going to do about that?

15. the valuing

"I'm telling you: marriage is the Jack Kevorkian of romance."
- friend's comment in The Story of Us

Have you noticed how most romantic movies are about unmarried couples? All the passion, all the bliss of the unknown, all the excitement in a relationship are portrayed when the couple first meets and dates—or has an extramarital affair.

Chances are, if you have watched any movies or television lately, you have seen unmarried couples making out. If the Nielsen television ratings and Oscars are any proof, you would think that unmarried relationships have the corner on romance and passion.

Occasionally, these relationships lead into marriage. "Happily ever after" may begin when a couple pledges their enduring love to one another—but then the credits roll. Rarely do we see on television, on the big screen or in real life what that looks like. What *does* romance in REAL marriage look like anyway?

Think about it. When was the last time you saw a married couple on television who were passionately kissing, taking each other's clothes off and running for the bedroom? What was the last movie you watched that had a married couple hot for one another?

Marriage and sexual passion are usually mutually exclusive on screen. Unfortunately, this is often true in real life, too.

Just Plain Boring

A radical doctor made headlines in recent years by assisting people in killing themselves. Dr. Jack Kevorkian, also known as Dr. Death, illegally helped end the lives of many painfully ill people (before he went to prison for doing it). At least for a few years, if you wanted to end your life, then all you needed to do was go see the doc.

In the movie *The Story of Us*, they call marriage "the Jack Kevorkian of romance." From this viewpoint, if you want to end your romance, then just get married. Marriage will kill any romance or passion you experience.

This does not bode well for marriage, in our opinion. It certainly does not give you much to look forward to on your wedding day.

If there is some truth in the analogy, however, we would say it is because marriages too often become predictable and boring. We quit taking risks to create new experiences with each other because we think we have done it all. We quit the chase to capture each other's hearts because we already have each other. We quit pursuing each other in new ways sexually because we reason we have already tried everything. In ways like these, typical marriages do kill romance.

Besides, marriage is expected to be boring, right? As one of our own daughters commented about us when we were holding hands one night, "They're not in love; they're married." We were stunned by her statement. Where did she get that perception? Had we somehow given it to her? While fantasy and romance are highly regarded, marriage is seldom viewed as utopia, even by married people.

We move on to careers, mortgages and babies; for a time, we find great satisfaction in these. If we admit it, though, we still want more. No matter how successful we are in life's endeavors, we still want to experience passion; to feel alive; to connect deeply with another person; to live out our fantasy. The problem is that we neglect trying to do these in marriage anymore.

At the lunch table in *The Story of Us*, when Katie and her friends discuss marriage and sex, this dialogue takes place:

> "I haven't made out—I mean, really made out—with Larry for years," one friend admits.
>
> "Doesn't that make you sad?" Katie asks.
>
> "Not really," her friend replies.
>
> "Why?" Katie presses.
>
> "I don't know," shrugs her friend.
>
> Their friend chimes in with her opinion,
>
> "It's inevitable. It's the wear and tear of the job ... the diapers, the tantrums, the homework ...
>
> "Finally you come face to face with the immutable truth that it's virtually impossible to French kiss the

person who takes the new toilet roll of paper and leaves it resting on top of the empty cardboard roll … I'm telling you, marriage is the Jack Kevorkian of romance … "

Maybe, as these friends discuss, the boredom, the never-making-out, the wear and the tear of the job *are* inevitable. Still, every one of us craves new experiences. We all like to get new things, see new things, go new places, eat at new restaurants, buy new houses and cars and clothes, hear new music and the list goes on and on and on. The new always creates comparisons with the old.

Do you ever go look at houses, then come home, look at your house and say, "Man, I wish we had a new house like the one we saw today." Have you ever driven by the car dealer-ship or ridden in someone's new car and commented, "Look at my ol' beater! I sure wish I had a new car!"? Have you ever gone to the mall and seen some new clothes, only to look at your wardrobe and think, "I sure need some new clothes"? Sure you have. You are created to desire new experiences.

This is why it is so easy for marriage to grow stale, boring and old. *Married couples often forget to bring new experiences into marriage.* Thus, the boring predictability becomes the killer of passionate romance in your marriage.

Once humdrum becomes habit, it is easy to become enamored by something or someone new somewhere else in your life. It is easy to meet a guy in an online chat room and get enamored by the "new to you" of his story. It is easy to meet a woman at work and become enthralled by her physical appeal.

When your marriage becomes predictable, you start looking for some way to do something new. Not getting enough sexual satisfaction from your spouse? Give it to yourself by masturbating while thinking about someone else. Tired of sex with your spouse? Try swapping spouses for a night. Tired of looking at your spouse's same old body? Watch some pornography. Ready to try a new level of excitement? Go for multiple partners—you will love it. The rationalizations abound.

We live in a day and age when there are a zillion suggestions for fulfilling your illicit fantasies, such as strip bars, X-rated movies and online pornography. Passion in marriage is easily replaceable in our society today, and our culture accepts this.

Not only can you find new passion outside your boring marriage, you can always find a new person, too. If your marriage is not striving to create new experiences, somewhere along the way, one or both of you will become intrigued, maybe even consumed, by someone new who is not your spouse. From our perspective, you will either have new experiences with your spouse or you will discover a new partner with whom you can experience something new.

Have you ever spent time with another couple and felt drawn to someone else's spouse instead of your own? Have you ever noticed a person you would like to experience passion with, someone who is not your spouse? Have you felt your heart drawn to someone besides the person you made your vows to?

You may not want to answer these questions, but we will. Yes, we have felt things like this. We are intrigued by new experiences. Not only do we want them, we crave them. The Creator designed us this way—to innately long for what is new. The Ancient Scriptures tell us that one day He going to make *all* things new. That is what Heaven is about, but this is what we are looking for in the here and now.

Should we feel bad about ourselves for desiring new experiences? Should we find new experiences outside the context of monogamous marriage? Or should we dig a little deeper and discover something new about our lives and marriage? We, most definitely, suggest the latter.

If our REAL love is going to continue to blossom and grow, we must continue the chase of discovering new ways to experience each other in marriage instead of new experiences outside marriage. Instead of buying a new car, polish the one you have. Instead of buying a new house, redecorate the one you own. Instead of looking for those new experiences with someone or something else, look for them with your spouse.

New Experiences

If marriage is the Jack Kevorkian of romance, then how do we keep passion alive as we *Love Each Other* in a REAL marriage? In the past two chapters of this section, we discussed the first two acronyms of love: "Lead in Love" and "Offer Yourself." These are foundational in love, but there is more. To love one another in a REAL way, we must also "Value New Experiences."

This is where the concepts of *REAL Marriage* come full circle. Instead of being the Jack Kevorkian of romance, marriage should be the greatest aphrodisiac of romance. Marriage can be where your greatest dreams are fulfilled and deepest passions are lived out. REAL marriage has its share of reality, for sure, but it balances that with a healthy portion of fantasy. When you love each other in a REAL way for a lifetime, you have the ideal opportunity to experience "happily ever after."

True "happily ever after" is not a dull and stagnant place, though. You will not stay there by simply remembering the happiness you used to have. You must pursue new arenas of enjoyment in your marriage in order for it to continue being "happily ever after." When you "Value New Experiences," you will discover that your fantasy and reality converge like never before.

So, what will happen when you "Value New Experiences"? We have a few thoughts on this.

You will come alive with new experiences. Not only do we all long for new experiences in our lives, we also need them because they counter-balance all the bad experiences. Every marriage will have its share of fights, sickness, disappointment, confusion and misunderstanding. New experiences make us feel alive and offset all the other negative things in our lives that make us feel dead.

Do you feel alive in your marriage? We must confess there are times that we do not. There are times we feel like we bring emotional death to each other instead of life. In spite of this—or maybe because of this—we keep seeking to bring life to each other through new experiences.

You help protect your marriage through new experiences. When you feel death in your marriage, you want to run from it. On the other hand, when you feel new life in your marriage, you will be drawn toward it. New experiences will bring life and vitality into your relationship. This is a protection, a safeguard for your marriage.

The moment you stop creating new experiences for each other is the moment you stop progressing positively with each other. This leaves you with only the negative of life and it eventually makes total sense why your eyes, heart and perhaps body might be drawn to someone other than your spouse.

A generation ago, the general consensus was, "Stay married because it is the right thing to do." People listened back then, but not so much anymore. You have to actively pursue your spouse because, if you don't, you can be assured that somebody or something else will.

Now, we are not suggesting that you be paranoid, fearful or insecure about this. We simply want you to recognize the issue so that, years from now, you do not have to be one of those people saying, "I don't know how it happened." We are telling you right now how it happens: without new experiences, your marriage will be unprotected.

When your relationship is struggling and you are tempted to walk down the path of having a new experience with someone else, no matter how innocent it may seem at the time, you should consider the potential outcome of the path. If you give up on your marriage, you are simply starting all over; you are not progressing. Eventually, you will grow bored and familiar with this new person as well.

Affairs and divorces do not "just happen." Neither does REAL marriage. You must be intentional about pursuing your spouse, creating new experiences and bringing new life into your marriage. This protects your marriage.

You will feel a greater satisfaction with each other through new experiences. We cannot tell you the number of times we have listened to a new song, bought each other new clothes, gone out to a new restaurant or driven to a new place when, at the end of the day, we felt a satisfaction with each other that we did not know prior to that experience.

New experiences with each other help us let down our guard, weaken our defenses toward one another and create a "mood" that is positive. Good moods are hard to come by. Bad moods are much more common because our minds are tempted to think only about the wrong, the bad, the shortcomings and all the other negatives that can and do come with a long-term relationship.

New experiences give us, quite literally, something new to think about. If you are dissatisfied in your marriage, then give it a vitamin boost of new experiences. You will never know what can happen until you try!

You develop greater fondness about past marriage memories with new experiences. A new experience also spices up the past. When you have new experiences with one another, it causes you to remember other good experiences you have had with each other. This can help you let go of the past negatives and cling to the past positives. Your present new experiences give you a satisfaction with your spouse in the present that enriches your view of your past.

Your long-term story is the most powerful thing you share with your spouse. No other person in the world knows this story as the two of you do. It is ironic that, though boredom and predictability are often born out of familiarity, so is fondness. You cannot have enriched fondness for one another without memories. The sweat and tears you have shed for one another now enshrine past experiences which once were new. These memories have added pages to your story that you can be proud of. These "thousand strands" are reminders of what you have together.

What is beautiful about marriage is that this history can create a future. When you are committed to the chapters of your past "story of us," you have a lifetime to work through the hard times or boring times and write new chapters together.

Certainly, past memories are not enough to get you through the present. However, they can remind you that you *have* a present—and a future. You seek new experiences for the life they remind you that you have already shared with your spouse as well as for the life they help bring into your current experience.

Ideas for New Experiences

In our opinion, marriage is *not* the "Jack Kevorkian of romance." If it was, then we would simply suggest that you avoid getting married and spare yourself the pain. The truth is that boredom, familiarity and staleness is a part of *every* relationship whether you are married or not. This is not a married condition; it is a human condition.

We believe that the real Jack Kevorkian of romance is not valuing new experiences. When you begin to value and create new experiences within your marriage, you will find a sense of destiny that will carry you through the stale times and inspire you during the hard times. We can draw the best out of each other in marriage through new experiences. These moments help propel us into REAL marriage.

Yes, this is a choice. But, really, it is more than a choice. It is being willing to see marriage as an adventure, not just a destination. Marriage is something you commit to, not arrive to. Marriage is something you explore and experience together for a lifetime.

Marriage is not only something you do; it is something you are. It is something you become. You and your spouse become a marriage; you become an "us." You become what you have experienced and keep experiencing.

So, if you don't like your marriage, don't change your spouse. Change your experiences. Sounds easy enough, right? It is easy, until your marriage is stuck in reality and cannot manage to grasp a shred of fantasy. Every marriage gets stuck at some point, ours included. Because of this, we have identified three categories over the years where we work to "Value New Experiences" in our REAL marriage. These three categories of new experiences are: everyday, exceptional and extraordinary.

The first category, "everyday ways to value new experiences," lists the types of things we do on a regular basis to stay connected to one another. There is nothing mind boggling about these; they are a normal part of the ebb and flow of our relationship. The everyday ways are simple threads of the "thousand strands" that connect our marriage.

The second category we call "exceptional ways to value new experiences." These are what we consider to be special ways that we connect with one another. These ideas are unique to us simply because they require effort. We have to go out of our way to make them happen. Some of the exceptional ways, like praying together, are weekly for us, while other ideas may happen once or twice a year.

The final category, "extraordinary ways to value new

experiences," contains many wonderful new experiences that may happen once or just a few times in a lifetime. These are extraordinary because they require extra, extra effort and because they extract a higher price in our relationship. The payoff, though, is as momentous as it is costly. The extraordinary things we do in our marriage earn the right to become the chapter titles in our "story of us."

In the following lists, we will share some of our own everyday, exceptional and extraordinary new experiences as well as some that other couples have shared with us. These are examples of how you can keep transferring passion and experiencing fantasy in your relationship.

Everyday Ways to Value New Experiences:

- Read a marriage book together.
- Go to church together.
- Go out on a special date. Try a new restaurant.
- Watch a romantic movie together that provokes both emotion and the desire to talk, connect and even make love.
- On your day off, sit and talk for a while before trying to get all the chores done. Make connection time the first item on your honey-do list.
- Go for a long walk holding hands.
- Listen to new music that provokes emotion and the desire to connect. Dance—even if you are not very good at it.
- Write a series of love letters to your spouse. Send random notes, cards, text messages or emails.
- Journal, then exchange and read each other's journals to better understand one another.

- Shop for new clothes as a couple. Go into the dressing room together and model the clothes for each other. (This always heats the coals of love for us!)
- Make love somewhere other than in your bedroom.

Exceptional Ways to Value New Experiences:

- Spend a weekend together at a hotel or bed and breakfast.
- Celebrate your dating, engagement and wedding anniversaries. For each occasion, talk about your top ten memories of that time in your relationship.
- Go parking. (Who cares if you get caught? You're married!)
- Spend an evening or weekend together alone at home. Arrange for the kids to be elsewhere so you can have some romance. (See the last bullet under "everyday" ideas!)
- Attend a marriage retreat or conference together.
- Break out your engagement and wedding pictures. Watch your wedding video.
- Start working out together on a regular basis.
- Worship together. Pray together as a couple.
- Start a new hobby together like hiking or running. Set a mutual goal of climbing a mountain or running a marathon together.
- Remodel your bedroom to create an enticing, romantic place. Move the computer, bookshelves and clutter out so that fantasy can move in. Adjust

the colors and lighting to make your bedroom a place you want to be.

Extraordinary Ways to Value New Experiences:

- Write a book together—seriously. Devote a significant portion of the year to chronicle your own "story of us." (This can become a priceless legacy for your children.)
- Make a baby or adopt one.
- Invest in something meaningful or significant for your home. Deliberate on your choice so that both of you are pleased.
- Consider plastic surgery in order to fix physical struggles or enhance your body. (See the addendum that discusses this idea.)
- Design, build or buy your dream house. Build sweat equity together!
- Take your children on a road trip of your story, going back to where you first met, had your first date and got married. Tell parts of your "story of us" along the way.
- Move somewhere new.
- Become entrepreneurs. What side business has always interested you? (You never know when that great idea might pay off!)
- Go on your honeymoon for a second time. Relive the blissful parts of it, and re-create the parts that may have been disappointing. Whatever the highs and lows of that original trip, indulge in your honeymoon experience again.
- Take the vacation you have always dreamed about having.

How do you feel after reading these ideas? Do you feel alive? What words come to mind when you think about new experiences? *Excited, energized, hopeful?* Did some of the suggestions get the wheels of your imagination going? What great ideas for new experiences are swirling between the two of you? For the sake of your marriage, live them! Experience them! This is not an option if you want a healthy marriage.

In REAL marriage, you *must* "Value New Experiences" with each other. These will not guarantee you a perfect relationship, but they will create windows into the heart of your spouse so you can see that person in new ways.

Although it is impossible to maintain continual newness in your relationship, new experiences give you a chance to take a break from reality, let down your defenses and share a part of yourself with the person you fell in love with. This is the best of fantasy because it is lived in the context of your reality. REAL marriage ignites romance in ways the world has seldom seen.

What's on your agenda?

For Discussion:

1. What past "new experiences" are especially meaningful to you? To your spouse? Go down memory lane and talk about these.

2. Plan a time when you can specifically discuss protecting your marriage. Have you seen the need? Have you *felt* the need? Discuss some new experiences that would help you protect your relationship.

3. What is an "exceptional" experience for our marriage may be an "everyday" experience in your marriage. Your marriage is unique, so go out on a date with the sole purpose of creating your own list of "everyday," "exceptional" and "extraordinary" new experiences for your marriage.

4. Together, make a plan for a new experience you and your spouse want to share in the coming days. This may be an "everyday," "exceptional" or "extraordinary" new experience. Dream about this with one another.

5. Plan a way to surprise your spouse with a new experience.

16. the embracing

"I've always been big on happy endings.
You see, to me the most romantic, beautiful love
stories ever were the ones where two people meet, fall in
love, and then, fifty or sixty years later, one of them dies,
and then a few days after that the other one dies because
they just can't bear to live without each other.
Not that that's such a good example of a happy
ending..."
– *Ben in* The Story of Us

We will never forget our first embrace as a couple. We will never forget our first kiss, our first touch and our first night together, naked in each other's embrace. These pages of our story are amongst the most meaningful moments of our lives together.

In our own "story of us," we will continue to seek romance and intimacy with each other the best we know how for the rest of our lives. We will always strive to love by: "Leading in Love," "Offering Ourselves" and "Valuing New Experiences" for the health and fantasy of our marriage. We always want to embrace each other.

Ultimately, though, solely embracing one another will not fulfill the deepest need of our hearts. What will complete our story in REAL marriage is "Embracing the Greatest Love Story" ever written.

Made for REAL

You see, as incredible as REAL marriage is, we were made for even more than that. And so were you. The Ancient Scriptures tell us that our Creator, who is God, made us in order to have REAL relationship with us. We were designed to be in relationship with Him.

What may surprise you is that Scripture actually uses the analogy of a husband and a wife relationship to refer to the relationship we can share with God. If your marriage has been a negative experience, then this may be a difficult analogy for you to grasp. On the other hand, if your relationship is REAL, then you know what this analogy speaks about the potential in your relationship with God.

The Ancient Scriptures tell us that one day God's Son, Jesus, will come back to claim His bride. In the Scriptures, God refers to us as His bride and Himself as our bridegroom. Men, you may not like seeing yourself as someone's "bride." Although I must admit that I am not crazy about that, either, what is compelling to me about the analogy is how much God desires a permanent relationship with me. I get that, because I remember how much I desired *my* bride when Tosha and I got married. I wanted nothing more than to be in a lifelong relationship with her. That passionate desire is what God has for each of us.

God made you to be in REAL relationship with your spouse and, even more importantly, with Jesus. The Bible tells us that in the beginning of time the first married couple, Adam and Eve, experienced perfect relationship both with their Creator and with each other.

Along the way, though, the couple decided to choose their own path at the crossroads, and they disobeyed God. They chose not to follow the guideposts and went their own route. Unfortunately, we all do this in life and marriage sometimes. Adam and Eve's disobedience caused disconnection and separation in the perfect relationship they had shared with their Creator and with each other. They were placed under God's judgment and expelled from the Garden of Eden.

This judgment strained their relationship, to say the least. Whatever fantasy they had experienced in the garden was gone. Never again would they feel connection with one another as they had back in the Garden of Eden. Throughout the Ancient Scriptures, one can read that all relationships have struggled in some capacity ever since. Pointedly, marriages have felt the impact of this judgment as husbands and wives have struggled to relate to one another ever since Adam and Eve.

Over thousands of years, people sought means to reconcile themselves to God and to one another. Nobody ever found a way, though. Humanity, it seemed, was forever separated from relationship with God and forever doomed to battle against each other.

The Way to REAL

Finally, when no other option was available and right at the perfect time, the Ancient Scriptures record that the Creator intervened on our behalf. The Holy Spirit of God impregnated a young woman named Mary, who was engaged to be married.

Can you imagine how that affected her engagement to Joseph? Can you think of how this affected their future marriage? In their culture, Mary looked like she had been immoral, either with her soon-to-be husband Joseph or in some other adulterous relationship. She appeared to have broken the guideposts which, as we discussed in section two, prohibit sexual relationships outside of marriage. In that day, being pregnant out of wedlock was punishable by death.

Fortunately for Mary, an angel visited Joseph and encouraged him to believe Mary's story of how she became pregnant. Joseph chose to stand by his fiancée, trust her amazing story and care for her. As a man who chose to *Embrace Spiritual Guideposts* established by the Creator, Joseph waited until they were married to engage Mary sexually.

In due time, the Son of God was born of His virgin mother and became the perfect Son of Man. The Ancient Scriptures tell us that Jesus grew physically as well as relationally with God and with people. He lived, walked, breathed, farted, burped, hiccupped, slept, wept and ate like we do. More importantly, Jesus experienced every temptation and struggle we face in our lives today.

After a little over three decades of life, Jesus began performing miracles and demonstrating His true identity. Remember, not only was Jesus the perfect Son of Man, He was also the Son of God. He was the flesh-and-blood representation of our Creator. He was God come to the earth. He was the God Man, understanding humanity's temptations and struggles in every way, and yet never giving in to sin.

Because Jesus was the only One never to sin, He was the only One who could deliver us from it. Only He could set us free from sin because only He had never been in bondage to it.

Jesus' sinlessness allowed Him to become the perfect sacrifice for our sins. The perfect life of Jesus was the only sacrifice that could satisfy the eternal penalty that the first married couple brought upon the whole world.

Jesus made the choice to give Himself as a sacrifice. He even told His followers that no one could take His life; He would lay it down freely. Jesus gave His life for us because He loves us and wants to restore us to the perfect embrace we were made to experience.

Around 34 a.d., history records that Jesus died on a cross. The Bible tells us He died to take away the eternal separation that exists between us and our Creator. Scriptures also tell us that, three days later, Jesus resurrected from death. This resurrection gave Him victory over our brokenness, selfishness and sinfulness.

The Ancient Scriptures state that over five hundred people saw Jesus eyeball to eyeball after His resurrection. As we would be today, they were amazed and in disbelief when they saw Jesus alive again. Yet, they had the opportunity to experience Him and feel His physical embrace.

This was not just any embrace, though. It was the embrace of perfect love lived out in REAL relationship. They experienced the very thing we all long for and try to experience in our lives and marriages. We want to wake up every day and feel the perfect, loving embrace of another person.

Unfortunately, no human can provide that perfect embrace for us. Even in a REAL marriage, in which both spouses are doing their best to *Realize the Cost, Embrace Spiritual Guideposts, Align Your Will* and *Love Each Other*, there will be failure. Ultimately, all humans will disappoint us somehow in relationship and marriage, because we are all imperfect. Only Jesus will never fail us.

Before He returned to heaven, Jesus told His followers that He was going away to prepare a place for His bride. Right now as you read this, Jesus is preparing a home for you to join Him someday in heaven.

However, like with any marriage proposal, you must accept this relationship that He wants to share with you today, tomorrow and every day for the rest of your life and then for eternity. You must receive His offer in order to experience His embrace.

Experiencing REAL

Up to this point in the book, REAL relationship was about the two of you: you and your spouse. This decision about a REAL relationship with Jesus is a choice that you must make for yourself, though. Your spouse cannot make it for you; not even Jesus will force it upon you. You have to choose whom you will "wed" yourself to; no one can make that decision for you. Are you ready to "Embrace the Greatest Love Story" of all time? Are you ready to experience REAL with the Lover of your soul? If so, we invite you to enter REAL relationship with Jesus today.

Having a REAL relationship with Jesus is not altogether different from having REAL marriage with your spouse. The starting point is the same for both: *Realize the Cost.* You know that there is a cost involved to experience REAL marriage. There is also a cost involved to be in relationship with Jesus.

The Ancient Scriptures tell us that Jesus said this about *Realizing the Cost* to follow Him:

> If you refuse to take up your cross and follow Me, you are not worthy of being Mine. If you cling to your life, you will lose it; but if you give up your life for Me, you will find it.
>
> Matthew 10:38–39

This is no easy task; it is no easy cost. No doubt about it, the price is extremely high. Yet, this is what Jesus requires of all who choose to follow Him. We must be willing to sacrifice everything to follow Him. That "everything" may include your plans for your life, your dreams and your hopes. Sacrificing everything may mean you have to lay aside your agenda and your ambitions.

In order to experience REAL relationship with Jesus, are you willing to pay whatever price He asks you to pay? You know the benefits of REAL because we have talked about these throughout the book. Do you want to experience this enough that you are willing to do whatever it takes to have

REAL? Are you ready to set aside your personal outline for your life and choose God's plan for your life? If you are, then you are ready to follow Jesus.

The cost, as you know from this book, is the foundation; it is the beginning. It is where we establish REAL relationships and marriages. Once we have decided that we are willing to realize and pay the cost that Jesus requires, then we are ready for the next step in relationship with Him. This is *Embrace Spiritual Guideposts.*

The Ancient Scriptures tell us that Jesus said this about *Embracing Spiritual Guideposts*:

> All who love me will do what I say.
>
> John 14:23

Jesus has guidelines for our lives to protect us from ourselves, others, as well as the enemy of our hearts and the evil forces of this world. The only way to discover the spiritual guideposts that Jesus has for us is to read the Ancient Scriptures.

We encourage you to get a copy of the Bible. An easy-to-read translation is the New Living Translation, which we have quoted from throughout this book. Once you have this, begin reading the four Gospels—Matthew, Mark, Luke and John—that record Jesus' words and relationships when He walked this earth.

As you read these spiritual guideposts, you will discover inside yourself that things begin to change. The Ancient Scriptures tell us that, at the moment we give our lives to REAL relationship with Jesus, the Holy Spirit comes to live

Kelly and Tosha Williams

inside of us. The Spirit helps us live the way the Creator designed us to live.

As you feel these nudges and tugs in your heart to change, you will want to resist, though. This leads to the third step in REAL relationship with Jesus Christ, which is *Align Your Will* to your Creator. The Ancient Scriptures tell us that Jesus said this about *Aligning Your Will* to Him:

> If any of you wants to be My follower, you must turn from your selfish ways, take up your cross, and follow Me.
>
> Mark 8:34

We talked a lot about this verse in earlier chapters, so you know what it implicates in marriage. That same commitment—even more—is required in your relationship with Jesus. This is a lifetime commitment. "Turning from your selfish ways" is not easy, neither with your spouse nor in your relationship with Jesus. Selflessness requires sacrifice, sacrifice that emulates what Jesus did for us.

Jesus' cross symbolizes sacrifice for others. He asks us in marriage and other relationships to "take up your cross," that is, to bear burdens on behalf of others. As you live selflessly and bear these burdens, Jesus asks you to follow Him. The logical question is, *where?* God does not get that specific in Scripture. He simply wants us to acknowledge Him as our authority and to pattern our lives after His.

Certainly this is no easy task at times, especially when struggles and temptations come our way. Jesus' death on the cross was not an easy task, either. He chose, nonetheless, to make this sacrifice for us. Are you willing to follow His example and sacrifice for others?

If you are—if you choose to *Realize the Cost*, *Embrace Spiritual Guideposts* and *Align Your Will* to your Creator— then you will begin to look outside yourself for other people to love. This is the final letter of REAL: *Love Each Other.* The ultimate way to experience REAL is to pass it on to somebody else.

In the end, this is what we believe our earthly relationships are all about. We exist not only for marriage; we exist for the opportunity to love Jesus and then to love others into a REAL relationship with Jesus. You will love people better once you have experienced and then imitate your Creator's love for you.

Finally REAL

For the two of us, a REAL relationship with Jesus Christ is the glue that holds our marriage together. A REAL relationship with Jesus is the bond that enables us to bail water when life is tough, to bear burdens on behalf of each other and to lead each other by keeping our vows. REAL relationship with Jesus is, ultimately, what enables us to experience REAL with each other. This relationship with Jesus governs everything about our lives. His spiritual guideposts direct how we function and treat one another in marriage and in every other relationship.

Jesus has loved us. This love gives us the ability to *Love Each Other* in greater and greater ways. We believe that our marriage is one of the best ways for us to understand the love and the relationship that Jesus generously offers us. This gives us hope in our times of trouble. It gives us peace in times of confusion. It gives us direction in times of chaos. It gives us purpose in times of being broken by each other's selfishness and poor choices.

We believe that without Jesus it is not possible to maintain REAL marriage for a lifetime. Sure, you can love each other. However, in the end, it takes more than human love to complete the REAL story of a marriage. It takes the love of Jesus.

We invite you to "Embrace the Greatest Love Story" ever written: the story of Jesus and you. A relationship with Jesus has made all the difference in our own lives and marriage, and we know that REAL relationship with Him will make all the difference in your life, too.

In REAL marriage, "Fantasy Meets Reality" best when both of you are embraced by Jesus Christ and share that embrace together.

When you turn out the lights tonight, hold each other's hands and say, "Jesus, we want Your embrace in our marriage. Please make Yourself REAL to us!"

No earthly fantasy could ever offer the embrace that Jesus wants to give you.

afterword

As *The Story of Us* concludes, Katie and Ben sit on their sofa discussing the state of their marriage. With his arm playfully dangled around her shoulder, Ben poses a question to Katie:

> "I've got another game. I'm thinking of seven words. What are they?" Ben asks.
>
> " ... So they can be any seven words in the English language? Fair enough ... " Katie engages him, and she begins guessing those seven words. "And they lived happily ever after," she speculates.
>
> "That's six words, but you're very close," Ben smiles at her.
>
> "And they lived mostly happily ever after," Katie grins, as she looks at her husband through new eyes. "I hope so," Ben says.
>
> "I think so," Katie flirts. "Think so?" he queries.
>
> "I do," she responds. "I do, too," he agrees.

When the movie is over, Katie and Ben still do not have a perfect marriage. Yet, they have come to a place where their "story of us" is the most valuable thing in the world to them. Through the ups and the downs, the highs and the lows, they know that the chapters they have written are irreplaceable. So, they lean into their marriage and write more pages to their story, even if those pages could use some editing.

When you finish this book, we do not expect you to have a perfect marriage, either. Indeed, even after going through the concepts of this book, writing it and editing it over and over again, we do not have a perfect marriage.

Nonetheless, even amidst the reality of our lives, we agree with Ben and Katie that we live "mostly happily ever after." We have good days, and we have bad days. However, we get to choose the fantasy in our marriage every day.

This dance between fantasy and reality is what REAL marriage is all about. Every day that we keep working on this dance, our story becomes more wonderful to us as "Fantasy Meets Reality." We hope the same thing occurs in your marriage.

If *REAL Marriage* impacts your life, please recommend it to others. Also, we would like to hear about what has happened in your marriage. Please send us an e-mail at kelly@ vanguardchurch.org and tell us your story!

Kelly and Tosha Williams

addendum

Plastic Surgery

In chapter fifteen, we discussed how important it is for your marriage to "Value New Experiences." We put forth a list of ideas you and your spouse might consider to introduce new experiences into your relationship.

One idea we suggested was plastic surgery. Certainly, this idea raises eyebrows for some and draws cheers from others. Whatever your personal reaction to plastic surgery, it is, without a doubt, a hot topic in our society. Plastic surgery is the craze of our day. Mostly women do it, but plenty of men are in on the action as well.

Is plastic surgery immoral? Is it wrong to undergo breast augmentation? Is it sinful to alter your body for the pleasure of your marriage? Is it wrong to surgically correct a physical trait in order to increase your self-esteem with your spouse?

These are not easy questions to answer, but we believe they need answers. Elective plastic surgery is a very real option in our society today. If you have not considered it after watching *Extreme Makeover*, we bet you at least have a friend who has. The dilemma of whether or not it is okay is a dilemma with which many wrestle.

Not too many years ago, people were asking whether it was okay to use contraceptives like the birth control pill. Some in religious circles condemned birth control (and still condemn the practice today). In general, though, both society and religious circles have accepted the practice of birth control.

We have friends who tell us that they were frowned upon just fifteen years ago for giving their children dental braces. The concept of altering children's bodies, even if that was merely re-aligning teeth, was considered wrong because many believed you should not change anything about your body.

Most all of us today would say that is crazy. It is now generally acceptable in society and religious circles to look the best you can.

Elective plastic surgery has not entered that category yet, at least not in religious circles. It is not something you talk about in church too often. It certainly is not something you would express a desire for or admit you have experienced. Why? We believe there are many reasons, including fear of rejection, embarrassment, insecurity and shame from the body parts concerned. There is also the looming question of the morality of the practice.

Kelly and Tosha Williams

Because of this, we want to address this topic of plastic surgery. Is it okay or not okay?

We would like to answer that question with two bigger picture answers. Put "elective plastic surgery" into the broader category of "new experiences for your marriage." Really, the plastic surgery issue is like any questionable idea that fits into this category. In order for plastic surgery or any other new experience to be healthy and beneficial for your marriage, we believe that it must pass through two sets of tests before you engage in it.

The first test negatively answers the question of whether a new experience is appropriate.

A New Experience for Your REAL Marriage is Not Okay When ...

- The experience is void of reality.
  - A new experience is void of reality when it is impossible to experience it regularly in your marriage without it being destructive to one or both of you.
  - For example, you may want your wife to do something sexually that harms her physically. This creates a feeling of disappointment and failure, which will lead to the deterioration of your intimacy rather than the enhancement of it.
- The experience does not have your spouse's approval or acceptance.
- The experience includes a third party besides you and your spouse.
  - This includes *anything* that brings a third

party into your sexual relationship, whether that is a person, a page, a picture or whatever else you might think of.

- The experience is born out of an addiction or a comparison to another person.
  - Illicit fantasy is something reality cannot compete with because that kind of fantasy is completely selfish and self-seeking. This is everything that REAL marriage is not.
- The experience is not appropriate or timely for you or your spouse.
  - For example, maybe you want your wife to say or do something that is embarrassing given the context or inappropriate given the audience. This could include things like what you ask her to wear, say or do in the company of others.
  - If the new experience is not timely or appropriate for both of you, then what do you do? You must let that new experience lie dormant until your relationship or spouse can handle it or until the situation is appropriate for it.
  - *Both* spouses must be able to handle the new experience for it to be timely and appropriate.
- The experience is purely selfish and does not in some way seek pleasure and fulfillment for both of you.
- The experience does not make both of you feel loved.
- The experience is expected to create a connection you do not already have in your marriage.

- For example, while a physical alteration may enhance the intimacy of your sex life in marriage, it will not create intimacy. You are fooling yourself if you think it will.
- The new experience is solely for the purpose of money.
- The new experience violates *any* spiritual guidepost in the Bible.
  - The sexual guideposts are described in detail in chapters six and seven of this book.
  - Obviously, the Bible has many other guideposts that guide us through life. A study Bible with cross references can help you find answers about other types of experiences you may be considering.
  - There is a distinction between what the Bible actually says and what people interpret it to say. You have to proceed very carefully when you step into "grey areas" that are not specifically addressed in Scripture.
  - Seek spiritual guidance if you are confused about what the Bible teaches about a certain issue in your life or marriage.

In our opinion, a new experience in your marriage is not okay if it meets any of these negative criteria. If you choose to pursue this new experience anyway, you will be stepping outside the safety of the spiritual guideposts. Your marriage will ultimately suffer because of this.

For the sake of your marriage, do not pursue a new experience that cannot pass the first test. However, if you put your idea through the first test and it passes, then we encourage you and your spouse to consider your motivations in this next test.

What is Your Motivation for a New Experience?

- Does your motivation for this new experience violate any aspects of the first test?
- Do you or your spouse have unmet needs that you are trying to fulfill through this new experience? If so, what are they? *Should* these unmet needs be fulfilled by a new experience, or should they be met in another way in your relationship?
- Will you act, dress, live or relate differently after you have this new experience? If so, how? Will you be able to do so with confidence that you are doing what is right?
- Will you be able to maintain this new experience in the enhancement of your relationship?
- Are you hoping that this will change your spouse's view of you? If so, how?
- Can you honestly articulate to one another why you want the two of you to go through this new experience?
- Can you afford this new experience financially without jeopardizing your family's financial future and without sacrificing your ability to be generous?
- What are the potential risks and consequences, if any, that are associated with this new experience? Have you considered the idea thoroughly, understanding the complications and potential pitfalls of it?
- Can you engage in this new experience without

Kelly and Tosha Williams

violating your conscience or your spouse's conscience?

After going through these motivation checks, how does your idea for the new experience line up? Are your motivations noble for your marriage? Does the new experience still appear worthwhile? Then pursue it.

Whatever new experience you are considering, put it through the two tests we have described. Maybe you are considering a move to another part of the country, away from family and friends. Put your decision through this test. Perhaps you are considering building an addition to your house or taking a month-long family trip. See if the new experience you are contemplating can face the challenge of the hard questions.

So, let us go back to the issue of elective plastic surgery. Scriptures say,

> You do not belong to yourself, for God bought you
> with a price. So you must honor God with your body.
> 1 Corinthians 6:19–20

According to this verse, the stakes are high when it comes to your body. It belongs to God, and He requires you to honor Him with it. There is nothing questionable about this expectation; it is very clear. What is questionable is what exactly does or does not honor God. Is plastic surgery something that dishonors God? The Ancient Scriptures are silent about this. Nowhere does Scripture say you should not get plastic surgery; nowhere does it say you should.

The only Scripture that remotely refers to plastic surgery such as breast augmentation is:

> Let your wife be a fountain of blessing for you … Let her breasts satisfy you always.
>
> Proverbs 5:19

Now, if your spouse gets a boob job via a credit card, then they are not your spouse's boobs until you pay for them. It will not be "her breasts" satisfying you if they still belong to the credit card company! So make sure you do not buy plastic surgery on credit!

All joking aside, engaging in a new experience such as plastic surgery must be done with the conviction that you are ultimately honoring God with your body. Whether you or your spouse are considering a breast augmentation, nose job, chin lift, tummy tuck, breast reduction or anything else, you must reflect upon all the criteria in the two tests and proceed with a clear conscience before your Creator

Indeed, no matter what new experience you are considering, you *must* have a clear conscience toward one another and your Creator in order for that experience to be healthy for your marriage. If you *cannot* sit down and discuss the two tests; if you cannot talk honestly about them together; or if your idea cannot pass both tests, then you and your spouse should not pursue the new experience.

If you *can* discuss these questions openly and both feel like your new experience passes the tests, then go ahead and pursue it. In the case of elective plastic surgery, we encourage you to wait a length of time before you pursue this new experience. Wait at least a year before you do it, maybe even as long as three years. If, after some time, you and your spouse still feel your endeavor is appropriate and passes the tests, then go ahead and have this new experience in your marriage.

New experiences are a dance as delicate as the dance of vulnerability. There is not always an easy, cut-and-dry way to go about new experiences. However, they must be an intrinsic part of your REAL marriage in order for it to thrive.

Carefully weave some new experiences into the chapters of your "story of us." New experiences can be breathtaking ways that "Fantasy Meets Reality" in your REAL marriage.